STITCH
DISSOLVE
DISTORT

with machine embroidery

Valerie Campbell-Harding & Maggie Grey

STITCH
DISSOLVE
DISTORT
with machine embroidery

Valerie Campbell-Harding & Maggie Grey

BATSFORD

Acknowledgements

Our thanks to Michael Wicks for his wonderful photography, to friends and students for allowing us to photograph their work, and to Janome and Brother for the loan of sewing and overlocking machines.

First published in the United Kingdom in 2006 by
Batsford
151 Freston Road
London
W10 6TH

An imprint of Anova Books Company Ltd

ISBN/10 0 7134 89960
ISBN/13 9780713489965

A CIP catalogue record for this book is available from the British Library.

10 9 8 7 6 5 4 3

Reproduction by Classicscan, Singapore
Printed by Craft Print International Ltd, Singapore

This book can be ordered direct from the publisher at the website:
www.anovabooks.com

Or try your local bookshop

contents

Rainforest. *The Embellisher machine was used on felt to produce a softly coloured background with silk and wool tops in green and gold. The central area was then heavily stitched and embellished with fibres to form the central leaf. Folds were made and embellished to hold them together before dyed silk pods were stitched over the folds.*

introduction

So many new materials are available for embroiderers to use on fabric; in that excitement, it is easy to forget how important stitch can be. The new materials are changing the look of current work to such an extent that the stitch is overwhelmed by the material or technique that is being used.

This book examines some new and exciting ways to stitch, dissolve, melt and distort fabric, both before and after stitching. All the methods used are safe and this book will help you to understand the tools, materials and stitches needed for each section. Ideas such as altering the tension or working on both the back and the front of the fabric offer greater variations. The use of stitch is paramount; it underlies every process. The first section of the book examines ways of working with stitch — and altering and distorting it.

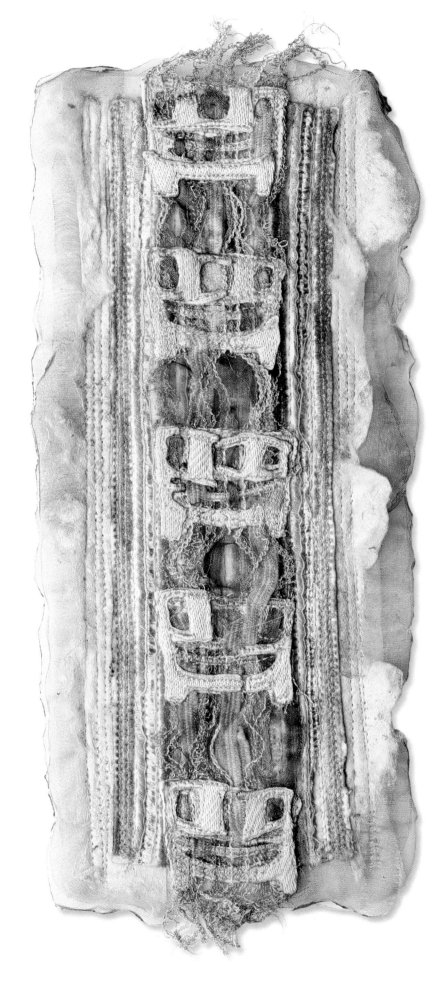

A panel with silk 'paper' on organza, with layers of knitting ribbon and pre-stitched motifs, secured with quilting stitch and free running stitch.

part one

stitch

In this section we return to our roots, looking at the amazing variety of imaginative work that can be produced using the sewing machine. Ideas are offered for both free stitching and incorporating the utility or built-in stitches. This section covers the following techniques.

- A new look at much-loved machine embroidery techniques, such as free running, whip and cable stitches. Used in conjunction with ideas for generating marks, from kebab sticks to rubber stamps, free machine enthusiasts will find much of interest here.
- Painted stitching. This is not just a good way to redeem a disaster, it can be a most exciting way of integrating work, can add texture and, with the introduction of emulsion paint, provide a gentle means of softening colours.
- Varying the weight of the thread, which can give results that are subtle and intriguing or bold and invigorating. This section of the book explores a variety of effects using this technique.
- Using an overlocker or coverlock machine. We were surprised to find that many stitchers have one of these tucked away in their workroom. We hope to tempt you to dig them out and try some of our ideas.
- Imaginative ways to use the utility stitches and built-in patterns, which can create a wonderful effect when distorted. We get away from the 'rows of stitches' look to find texture, shape and form – all with the foot on.

Free Machining

If you are new to machine embroidery, several good books are available. Look in your library or contact one of the embroidery suppliers. They will help you to master this exciting technique. At its most basic, just drop the feed dogs and use a darning foot (your machine manual will tell you how to do this). Then place the fabric in a frame, making sure that it is tightly held by the frame. Now practise stitching back and forth, guiding the frame as you stitch. Try heavy stitching for a massed effect and light lines as a contrast. This stitch is called free running stitch. Try it with a zigzag for a satin stitch effect.

Marks and Stitches

Making marks on paper using a variety of tools can suggest stitching that is unlike anything you have done before. Try dipping a kebab stick into ink and make marks using both ends. Now break the stick in half and use the broken ends to make marks. They are likely to be quite different. Then try using stalks of flowers, a brush, a feather or a calligraphy pen.

These marks can be translated into free stitching using mainly straight and satin stitch or could be scanned into your computer and then digitized for controlled stitching. The results are unique and they can be used in future pieces, building up patterns which can cover a surface, or used as the centre of attention over background stitching. Build up a stock of these, pasted into a small book, so that you can refer to them every time you are not sure what sort of stitching to do.

Marks and lines made using poster pens with multiple nibs.

A strip was taken from the centre of a drawing of an African body painting (in walnut and black ink) and woven with strips of stitched organza. It was stitched again to secure.

Cloth with cross-hatched stitching on the base fabric, with areas worked on the Embellisher (see page 93). Motifs were stitched, copying one of the stamps in the figure below, and laid over crumpled organza.

Below: Marks made using Sherrill Kahn's rubber stamps, which can be translated into free embroidery or scanned into the sewing machine software and stitched.

Stitching from Stamps

Rubber stamps, either commercial ones or those you have carved yourself, can be used for mark making; many of the commercial ones are based on lines, grids or textures. When printed on paper, they can suggest ways of stitching that you may not have thought of before.

The stamps are usually quite small but can be enlarged, either on a photocopier or after being scanned into your computer. If you are using them as small embroideries, think of stitching areas of free running as a solid filling or a loose hatching for some of the shapes. Narrow satin, whip or cable stitch bands can then be worked on top or around them to add emphasis. If you are doing larger samples, pieces of fabric or cut-up bits of stitching that have been worked previously can be applied with wider satin stitch or more rows of cable stitch worked over them.

One problem is that many of the lines are disconnected and machine embroidery, by its nature, is made up of continuous lines. The way around this is to lift the pressure foot at the end of every line and drag the thread to the beginning of the next one. You can leave the dragged threads as part of the pattern. If you are doing blocks of satin stitch, or 'beads', then the dragged thread is hardly noticeable. An alternative would be to change your machine setting back to straight stitch and just stitch from the end of one line to the beginning of the next. The small straight stitches will barely show.

A print could be scanned into your computer software and then digitized and stitched. You can work multiple repeats, cut them out of the background and lay them over another background of painted and torn or cut fabric shapes.

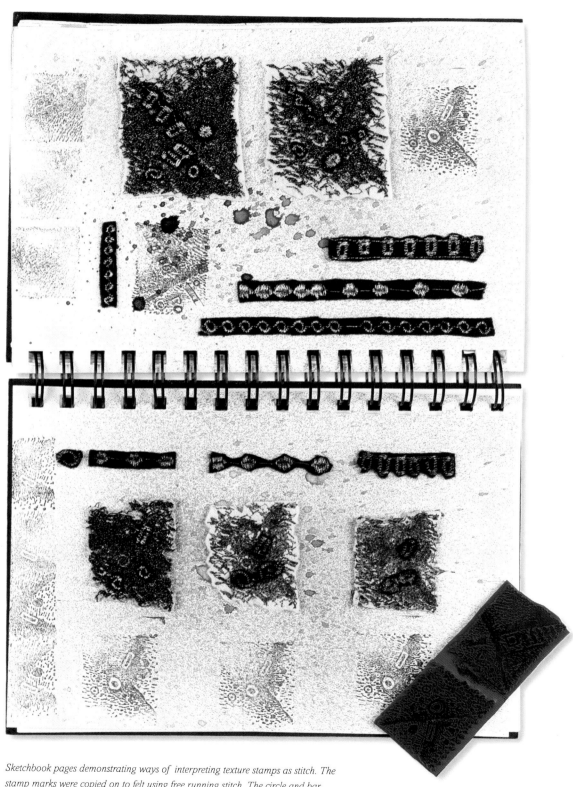

Sketchbook pages demonstrating ways of interpreting texture stamps as stitch. The stamp marks were copied on to felt using free running stitch. The circle and bar marks were stitched as eyelets and buttonholes. These were applied later by hand.

Above: Marks made using a feather dipped in ink.

Right: A detail of a scroll showing stitched marks.

Using Free Machining for Texture

We have noticed that the textured stitches, such as whip, cable or moss stitch, are not often used nowadays. This is a pity, as they can add so much variety to free machine embroidery and can give a real boost when used in conjunction with pattern stitches or free running stitch. Whip stitch is worked with a tight top tension and may require a looser bobbin tension. Some modern machines do not lend themselves to changes in the bobbin tension, so try making the top tension really tight for whip stitch. Also, try a variety of threads. Loosening the top thread and working upside-down is another option. Transfer the design to a backing fabric such as Stitch and Tear, place this under your fabric and turn it all upside-down. Now follow the lines and remember to have an interesting thread in the bobbin as it will show on the top.

If you can change the bobbin tension then work right side up. Experiment with the following:

- Keep the bobbin tension slightly loose and change the tension of the top thread. This can have surprising results, especially if one of the threads is the same colour as the background fabric. Parts of the stitch are lost as the threads twist around each other, which can distort the look of any stitching. Look at the back from time to time to see whether it is even more effective that way round.

A scroll with stitched marks applied over a variety of fabrics with massed straight stitching and couched gold thread.

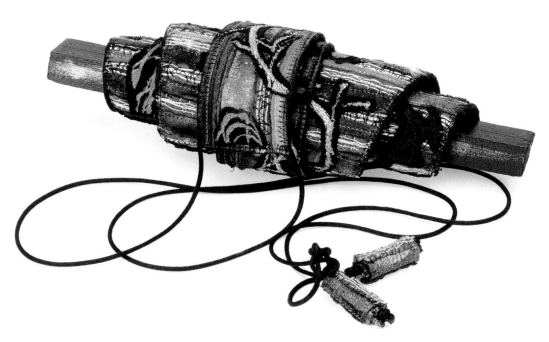

Above: The rich texture of moss stitch contrasts with open areas of fabric and coiled ribbon.

Right: An automatic sewing machine pattern, using blue thread, was worked on tissue paper bonded to calico. It was outlined with whip stitch in bronze.

Opposite page: Organza was laid over calico and stitched with quilting stitch. A heat gun melted the organza in places. A lace edging, worked on water-soluble fabric, was pleated and sewn to the edge. Separately stitched flowers were applied using free running stitch in yellow ochre and whip stitch using red thread.

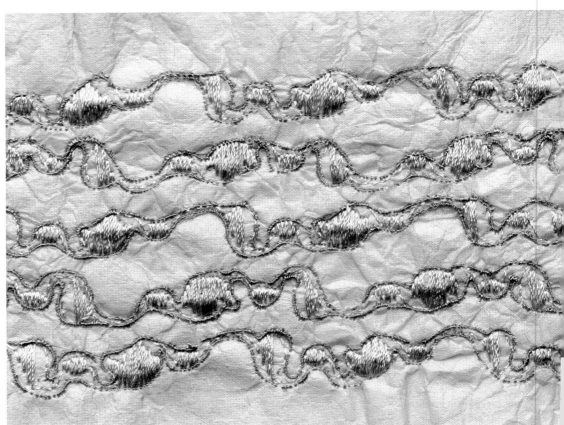

- Try winding several threads together onto the bobbin. These will wrap themselves around the top thread to give an effect that is almost like narrow cords. Make one or more of them metallic.
- Work moss stitch by loosening the bobbin tension even more to give a 'loopy' texture on the top. Then remove the top thread completely. Stabilize this by ironing Vilene on the reverse. It is possible to bypass the bobbin tension completely to give a very loose, loopy effect and this is worth a try. Moss stitch makes a wonderful background and invites further stitching on the top, perhaps using lettering or an automatic pattern.
- Work with heavier threads on the bobbin. This is 'trial and error' but most machines will accept quite thick threads if the bobbin tension is bypassed. Try perlé, knitting yarns, jap gold, fine braids and so on. Hand-wind the bobbins, if necessary, and make sure the winding is even. Try the built-in patterns with cable stitch too.

Free Stitching with Motifs or Patterns

The pattern stitches that are built into your machine can be exploited by stitching around them using whip or cable stitch. This adds emphasis and can be used to make the stitches look more prominent. It may also distort the pattern somewhat and make the result more interesting. It is particularly useful if your patterns are quite small. Free stitching can also be worked over digitized stitching, thus making it look less mechanical.

Work in rows or areas and leave sufficient room around the stitches to work the surrounding texture stitch. This is particularly effective with letters. Trace off some interesting letter shapes and free machine them, or use the lettering facility on your machine if you have it. Then surround the letter with free running stitch, tightening the top tension and/or loosening the bobbin to produce whip stitch. Turn the work upside-down and work cable stitch by winding a thicker thread on the bobbin. This will produce a weightier result.

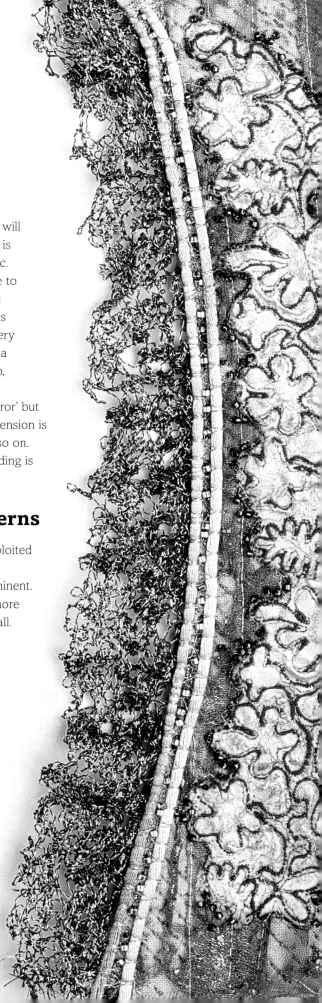

Encourage massed stitching to alter the texture and handle of the fabric and to provide contrast areas, such as working textured surfaces to set against plainer areas or heavy stitching with delicate, fine threads.

Any satin stitching, whether free or controlled, can be cut with sharp scissors so that the threads form texture, but this will need reinforcing on the back of the fabric, with iron-on Vilene or a bonded fabric, to prevent the stitches from falling out. Loops made using the looping or tailor-tacking foot can also be cut and then stitched over the top with free stitching; they too will need reinforcing.

Squares of rich fabric, applied with the quilting stitch, have built up the background in this textile. Some pieces of black net, stitched and melted, were laid down in parts. Finally, previously stitched motifs, based on ink marks, were applied with free running stitch.

Painted Stitches

Why would you paint some stitching that you have laboriously worked on? One reason may be that you like the look of painted stitches. Another might be because you dislike the colours you have used, or you might be faced with a complete failure – this happens to us all from time to time. The answer is to paint over the top.

It is also possible to obtain an excellent result by dyeing fabric after it has been stitched. Using a variety of natural or mixed-fibre fabrics will result in subtle differences in the way the dye is taken up. Easier still, use silk paints. Dampen the fabric first. Try colour sprays such as Pebeo's Tagger or the Ranger Adirondack sprays.

Flower-shaped marks, made from a fan brush, were stitched on felt and cut out. They were laid on a backing of felt, with areas of stitching worked on water-soluble fabric, and stitched to secure. The whole piece was painted with black acrylic paint. Gold and copper paints were stroked over the surface to highlight the texture.

However, for a more dramatic effect you can use acrylic paints, thick fabric paints, gesso or household emulsion. The emulsion is particularly effective because you can paint over the top with gentle colours. Allow the emulsion to dry and then paint over the top with any of the following:

- Writing ink, such as black Quink, goes a lovely shade of pale blue as you put it on, and then looks wonderful rubbed with other colours or metallic rub-ons.
- Black or burnt umber acrylic paints give a good base on which to rub oil painting sticks, or metallic rub-ons over the high spots, which emphasize the texture.
- Metallic paint – gold is usually great, but don't forget silver or copper too.

Just use any fairly stiff old brush, not a soft water-colour brush. Keep the paint fairly thick and dab, brush and press it into the surface so that it is completely covered. Sometimes you need two coats of white emulsion if the colours of the stitching are strong, so let one coat dry before you add the second. Or you may wish to leave the original colours showing through. You could use a second colour to highlight the pattern or some raised areas, putting this on when the first colour is dry.

A scroll with very textured embroidery, using different fabrics and pieces of stitching, was painted with white emulsion paint and then black writing ink that turned blue. Gold paint was stroked over some areas, and some were darkened with acrylic wax.

Detail from scroll shown on opposite page (top).

Above: The background is made of tiny squares of different fabrics stitched together, painted and stencilled with bronze paint. The central strip was made of gold stitching with tiny buttonholes worked at intervals and threaded with a zig-zagged cord. The whole piece was painted with white emulsion and tipped with gold paint.

Tone and Texture

Whether you are working in free or controlled
stitching, it is tempting to use the same colour or
thickness of thread all the time. However, the result
will look quite flat with not much change of tone. The
usual solution is to change the thread colour, but why
not try changing the thickness of the thread instead?
Surprisingly thick threads can go through the needle,
and of course on the bobbin, so try anything you
have at hand, whether it is a conventional machine
embroidery thread or not. Try crochet threads or
those meant for hand stitching, or even a knitting
yarn, just to see what happens, or perhaps a random-
dyed silk thread or a rayon tassel thread that will give
a sheen contrasting with matt threads.

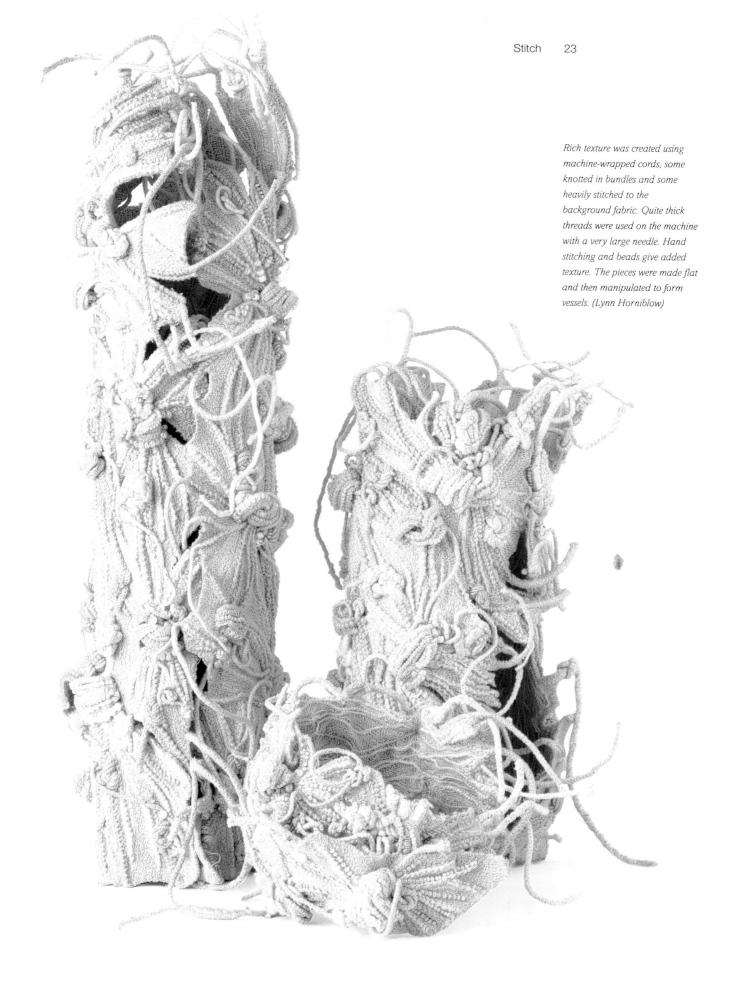

Rich texture was created using machine-wrapped cords, some knotted in bundles and some heavily stitched to the background fabric. Quite thick threads were used on the machine with a very large needle. Hand stitching and beads give added texture. The pieces were made flat and then manipulated to form vessels. (Lynn Horniblow)

Above: An automatic pattern – distorted, and using different thicknesses of line – shows tonal contrast.

Most machine embroidery threads come in size 40, and there are more colours in this size than any other. These threads are not the same as sewing threads and the sizes may differ. They are more loosely twisted, which gives a softer and more lustrous look to the stitch.

Some manufacturers produce a size 30 which is thicker than size 40 and, occasionally, a size 50 which is finer, but there is not usually as much colour choice. There are some thicker threads that will go through a size 100 or 120 needle or a size 16 topstitch needle and these will give variety.

A finer thread such as a bobbin thread, which is often size 80 or 90, is perfectly all right when used through the needle, although here again there is not much choice of colour. It comes on reels, cones or on pre-wound bobbins. The quality is sometimes not as good as it might be, and it can be hairy, so choose carefully. Another bobbin thread, which is equivalent to size 50/60 embroidery thread, comes in a wide range of colours, and can be used alone or doubled in the needle to mix colours. If you use one colour that is a contrast to the fabric you are working on, and one that is the same, you will get an uneven look to the stitch; this is enchanting.

For an even finer thread, look at lace threads which come in sizes from 100 through 120, 140, 160 and 180. It is very difficult to use threads that are finer than this. These threads are surprisingly strong but are almost always white, so think of doing white embroidery or painting the stitching afterwards. Change your needle to a smaller size and you might have to loosen the tension a bit. We sometimes use tension 2 or even 1½.

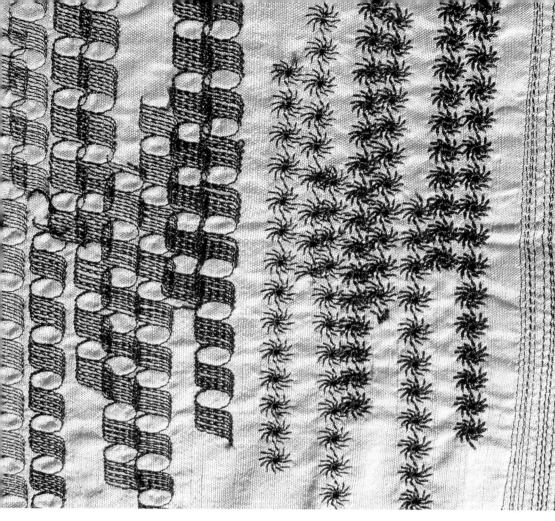

Machine embroidery threads in sizes 30, 40, 50 and 60 were used to give the tonal changes.

Machine embroidery and lace threads in sizes 90, 120, 160 and 180 give a much more delicate effect, especially on the back.

Using the Different Weights of Thread

We often turn our work over and are pleased with the way the stitching looks on the back. It may look more delicate, and sometimes more random, than when viewed from the front. Whenever you are stitching a piece, consider working on both sides of the fabric and stitch samples beforehand to see what this looks like. Try the following:

Below right: A computer design made by scanning the edge of a saucepan which was repeated and developed on the computer. (Sarah Brownie)

Below left: The saucepan design was printed out and used as a guide for free machining with different weights of thread. The lightest areas were worked upside down with perlé thread on the bobbin. White threads ranging from 40 to 180 were stitched on black fabric with grey machine embroidery thread to add the mid-tones.

- Draw a motif or trace one from a suitable copyright-free book. Make up a design by repeating the same motif, overlapping it in places. Transfer the design to tracing paper and lay it over your fabric. Stitch around the main lines and then pull the tracing paper away and discard.
- Stitch the motifs, working with a different weight of thread for each one. This can give interesting results. Overlap in places.
- Think about producing a design using different media to give the appearance of a change of weight. Interesting results could be obtained using black paper with white chalk and white crayons. Computer design programs can be a great help here. Reproduce this in a free machined piece, matching the thread weight to the depth in the design.

Overlock or Coverlock Machines

How many of us have one of these machines tucked away in a cupboard from dressmaking days? There are good reasons for working with them as they cover the fabric quickly. Many of the top-of-the-range machines also have a coverlock and chain stitch option. This type of stitching can look attractive when the fabric is dissolved. The machines will take a heavier thread on the loopers (lower threads). Many of them can also be used without fabric to make lacy braids. Massed stitched lines make a great base for further stitching. There is a lot to be explored with tensions on these machines, especially when loosening the looper tensions. Do try different combinations. Try different fabrics too: use felt and cut strips, or organza or net for a more delicate effect.

Samples made with the Janome coverlock machine. The tension was altered to produce lines of textured stitching on felt, which were then cut out and pleated or formed into braids. The machine has a very useful chain stitch option that looks good when the rows of stitching are massed together.

Thread up the machine with interesting thread, in particular experimenting with thread on the loopers. A heavier metallic thread (Madeira produce one called Glamour which works well but lots of threads of similar weight could be used instead) combined with a variegated silk or cotton used as the upper thread could be an exciting combination. Having found a good mix of threads, here are some thoughts and ideas that you may like to try.

Consider using the machine with dissolvable film or fabric, especially for some of the techniques for straight line stitching included in the 'Dissolve' section (page 52). The overlockers only stitch on the edge of the fabric, so use strips of dissolvable film. Overlockers with a coverlock facility (without the knife engaged) or coverlock machines will stitch anywhere on the fabric. When working the straight lines on soluble film, it is necessary to mass the lines of stitch for a good result. Overlock and coverlock machines can really speed up the process.

Opposite: The under layer shows strips of fabric held down with quilting stitch. The top layer is of black net stitched on a coverlock machine and then melted in places. Strips of pink fabric and threads were wrapped round small cork tiles to add emphasis. (Sandra Coleridge)

Below: Straight lines were stitched on organza and net with the coverlock machine, using a variety of threads and changing the tensions. The resulting fabric was made up into a cushion and a detail is shown here.

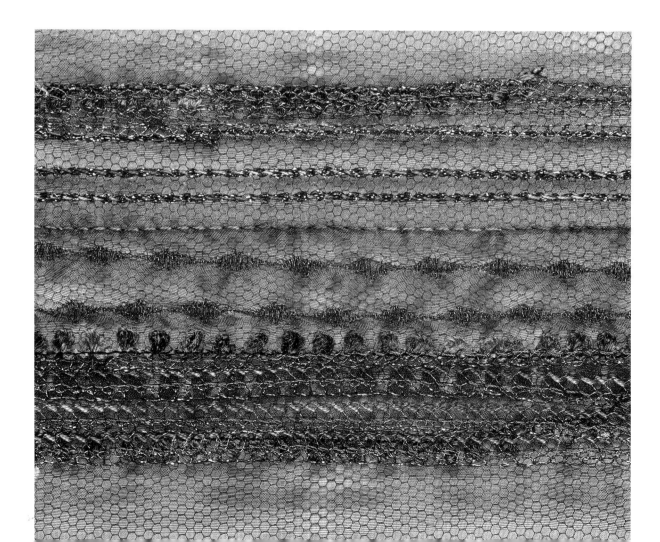

Close-up of coverlock stitching on Thermogauze that has been burnt away.

Try the following:

- Stitch on Thermogauze (vanishing muslin) over a base fabric, zap with a heat tool and paint after stitching.
- Stitch on felt and cut out the strips. Plait them and use as braids to decorate edges or bind multiple strips to use as tassels.
- The overlocker can produce wonderful cords very quickly. Try using the beading foot and running a cord or string through the machine and stitching over it. The correct tension is crucial so that the threads wrap the cord tightly.

Coverlock machine stitching, which gives a double row, was used to secure the knitting tapes and applied fabric pieces.

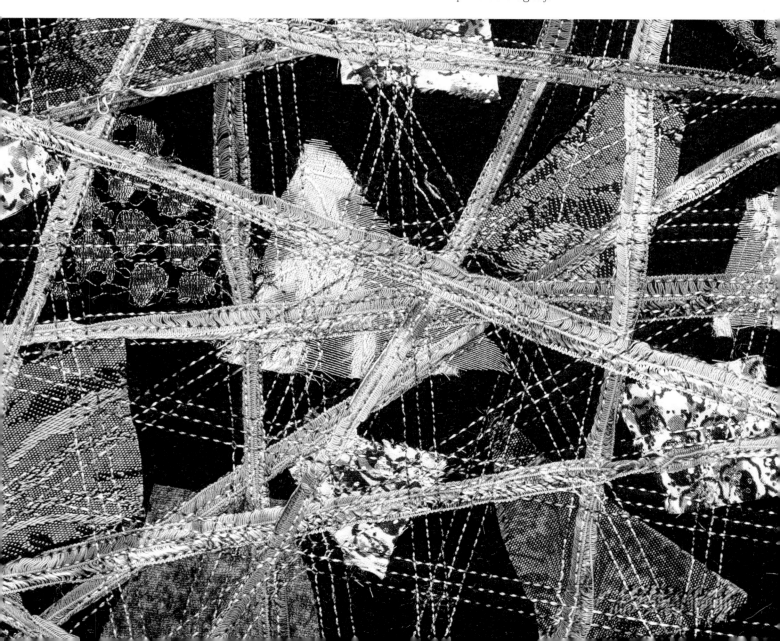

Spaghetti Bag. Lines of coverlock stitching on water-soluble fabric were dissolved and twisted into a swirl. This was applied to a velvet background and fashioned into a bag. The swirls were held down with a stitch here and there to avoid flattening them. Wrapped pipe cleaners add emphasis.

Pintucks

An excellent way to add texture and body to fabrics is to use the pintuck foot. These are available for all machines; the five-groove foot is the most useful and can be used with twin needle sizes 3, 4 and 4.5. If you are using a heavier fabric, a three-groove foot and a size 6 twin needle will give lovely big grooves.

If both the top and bottom tensions are slightly tightened, the tucks will be raised, so keep adjusting the tension until the desired result is achieved. Fabric that has been previously coloured, printed or stencilled can be fabulous when used with pintucks. Computer-printed fabrics work really well too. Try pintucking first and then stamping or stencilling afterwards. Designing for pintucks can be fun, especially if corrugated paper is used to represent the tucks.

Massed pintucks have been worked on a computer-printed fabric further decorated with blue stencilling.

A design for a pintucked vessel using corrugated paper, straws, curtain rings and lace bobbins. It was all painted black, with gold and blue metallic paint stroked over to emphasize the texture in places.

Massed pintucks, following the pattern on a printed fabric, contrast with a textured background with stitched and burnt Thermogauze, builders' scrim, and embossed shapes in white Modelight. Some threads made on an overlocker were applied and the whole secured with free stitching.

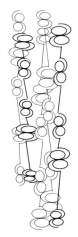

Zigzag, Utility and Built-in Patterns

Don't overlook the patterns and utility stitches on your sewing machine. They do tend to look very regular, so it is a good idea to aim for a distorted effect. Enormous opportunities await you when using them. The following pages will concentrate on a number of different methods.

Dragged Stitching

A good way to break up the built-in utility stitches or patterns is to stitch them with spaces between them. The threads will lie on top of the fabric and will form part of the pattern. Even if you have no patterns or utility stitches, this technique works well using basic zigzag stitching (increase or decrease the width as you stitch) or the Flower Stitcher attachment. Here is the basic method:

1. Leave the teeth up and use your standard foot and normal tension. Select one of the utility stitches or a narrow pattern.
2. Work two or three stitches, then lift the presser foot lever and move the fabric along a bit, dragging the thread.
3. Lower the lever, stitch one or more stitches and move along again. If you work with your left hand holding the fabric behind the needle and your right hand on the lever, you can work quite quickly.

When you have experimented to find interesting stitches, try some variations.

- Work in both directions and overlap the rows of stitches. This gives an interesting irregular effect.
- Try a thick fabric like felt or velvet and use a thread the same colour as the fabric. This will give texture to the fabric rather than obvious stitches.
- Try one thread through the needle, then two threads of different colours to make thicker stitches. Cable stitch, with a thick thread in the bobbin and turning the fabric upside down, gives an even thicker stitch.

Top diagram: Dragged and distorted stitching created from an altered automatic pattern put into the memory. When worked in two different weights of threads it gives a depth of tone.
Bottom diagram: The same stitching when worked over applied fabrics with a motif based on one of the marks shown on page 24 stitched on top as a centre of interest.

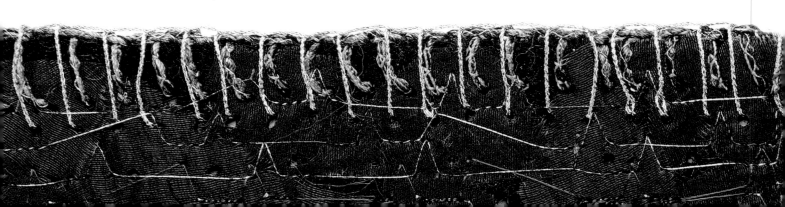

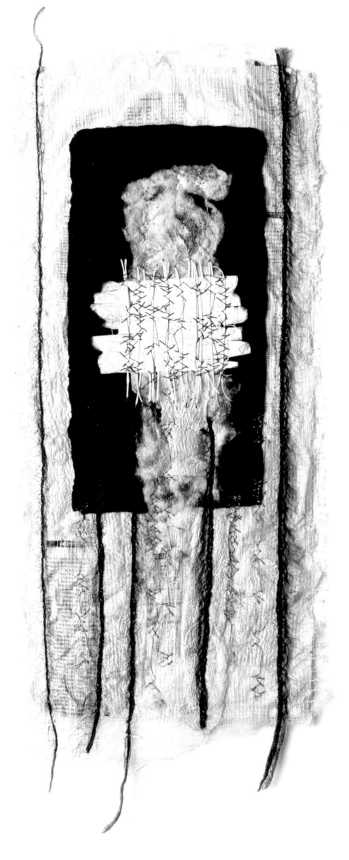

A panel using calico, builders' scrim, silk carrier rods, black felt, silk 'paper' and woven strips of paper, all secured with dragged stitching in fine black threads.

Opposite: A hand-stitched buttonhole edge worked on a piece with dragged stitching that secures overlapping pieces of organza.

- Work rows of built-in patterns, changing the stitch to give a variety. Select the thread to tone with the background fabric. Alternatively, stitch over the background using free machine techniques. Then turn the work over and stitch using the zigzag stitch with a heavier thread on the bobbin and fracturing the stitching.

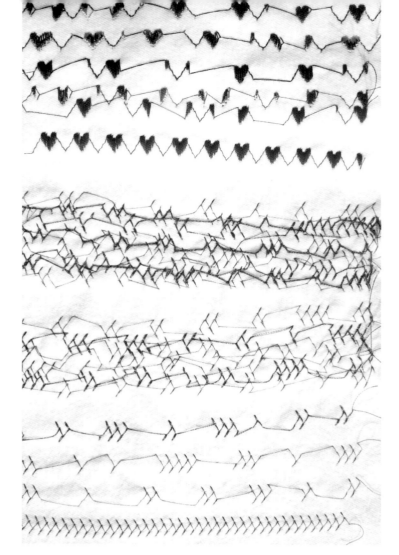

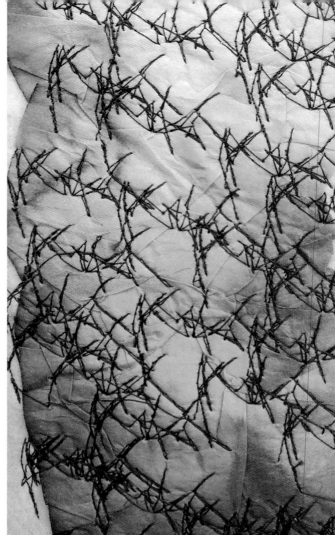

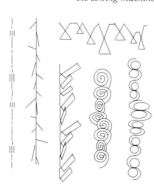

Distorted Stitches

This technique gives a less precise effect, more in keeping with textured surfaces.

These instructions will vary according to the machine you are using, so you will need to use your manual and find out how to put in a sequence of stitches. The following steps are based on that section of your own sewing machine manual.

Do not use any of the satin stitches as they are not really effective, but try the utility stitches and the more open linear patterns. Patterns that go forward and backwards as well as from side to side work the best.

1. Open your memory and choose an empty one to save the sequence.
2. Select a stitch, bearing in mind the points raised above. Put the stitch once into the memory and save it.
3. Select the same stitch. Alter the length quite a lot, say from 2 to 5. Add to the previous stitch in the memory and save it.
4. Choose the same stitch again and radically alter the width. Put into memory as before.

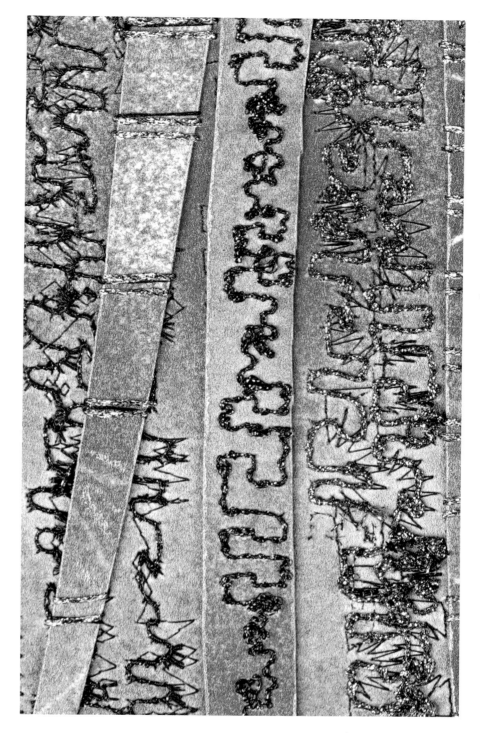

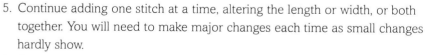

Above: Distorted stitching over
random satin stitch worked with
a thick thread on the bobbin. It
was then further worked with a
thick thread over random satin
stitch in a fine thread.

Left: Distorted stitching using a
thick thread on the bobbin and
working upside down. In some
areas this is worked over the same
pattern stitched in fine threads.

5. Continue adding one stitch at a time, altering the length or width, or both
   together. You will need to make major changes each time as small changes
   hardly show.
6. Continue until you have a reasonable string of varied stitches in the memory
   and then make a final save.

When this sequence is stitched on the fabric, it will repeat the length over and
over, so the more variations (which make a longer string) the better as the repeat
will be less noticeable.

This technique is useful for layering fabrics, altering the feel of a fabric and giving it more body, for texturing a surface and for appliqué.

To add even more texture, try pressing the reverse button every few seconds while you are stitching these bands. This will build up density and give an even freer result. Try this technique with all the built-in stitches as well, but remember to be careful with the satin stitch patterns as they may become congested. You could also use distorted stitching with different thicknesses of thread, as suggested on page 24. Try working on the back and the front, turning over to give a variation of tone.

The base shows red distorted stitching on calico. The finished piece was then embellished with gold tissue, scraps of red fabric and rows of quilting stitch.

Strips of the fabric opposite were cut and laid on a black backing fabric together with strips of frayed red fabric. A square of the stitched fabric was stitched in tucks that secured lengths of zig-zagged cord, knotted at the ends.

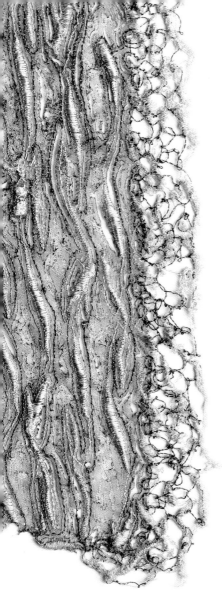

Elongated Stitches

Many machines have a facility for elongating or shortening the stitches. This is not the same as lengthening or shortening the stitches and is there so that you can match up rows of the built-in patterns. This is often described in the manuals as 'balancing the stitches'. Used creatively, it gives very free effects, even when stitching with the foot on.

Have a look in your sewing machine manual to see how to change the balance on your machine and set it up according to the instructions. Some machines will do as many as seven elongations, some only four, but they are not always calculated in the same way so you will just have to try it and see. Some machines will add stitches as you lengthen the patterns, while others will not, so if you find your pattern a bit empty-looking, use two threads through the needle to give a richer effect. You may have to alter the stitch length to avoid the stitches piling up on top of each other. Sometimes you will find that the patterns stitch themselves backwards as the result of altering the balance too far in one direction, but this can be exciting. Add to the effect by doing fractured stitches, as described earlier, moving the cloth between parts of the pattern, or putting the distortions made by altering the balance into the memory.

You can stitch in straight lines or gentle curves, or use single patterns at random over a surface, perhaps working in different directions. Try them on different fabrics: they will sink into velvet, and appear raised on a smooth fabric. Stitching them on water-soluble fabric makes them look even less defined and more like free machining.

An elongated pattern, worked on organza, showing movement and delicacy. A lace edging using water-soluble fabric stitched with the same elongated pattern is a contrast to the main piece. (Doreen Woodrow)

Quilting Stitch

This stitch is found on many machines and is a version of whip stitch which is already built into the system. It is the nearest stitch we have to a running stitch done by hand. It gives a broken line and is far less rigid than an ordinary straight stitch. Look in your manual to see if you have it (it may be called something else, but the icon for it is a single stitch and then a triple straight stitch). If you don't have the stitch then use the memory. Put these two stitches in a memory and then adjust the tension until you get the right effect.

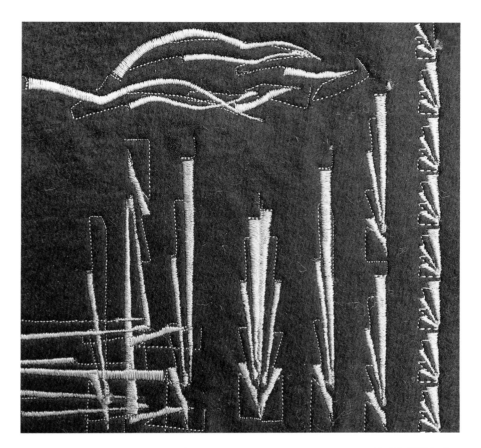

*An automatic pattern that has
been elongated up to seven times
and worked in curves and as a
corner design.*

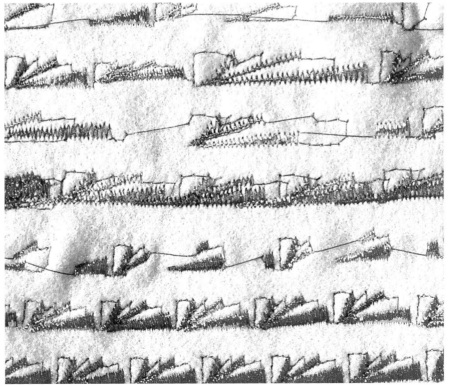

*The same elongated pattern stitch
with a variegated thread and
stitched in bursts using the
fractured stitching technique.*

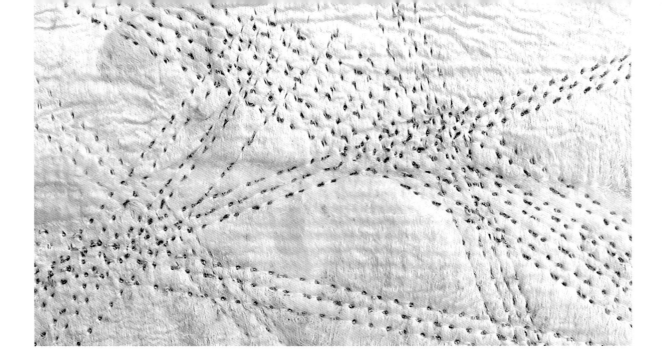

You should use a transparent nylon thread through the needle; the smoke colour looks better on many fabrics than the white one.

- Thread your machine as you usually do, with the coloured thread on the bobbin. This is the one that will show on the right side of the fabric. Leave the standard foot on the machine and the teeth up. On newer machines the tension will be set for you automatically, so don't alter it. On older machines, tighten the top tension.
- As you are stitching with the foot on, you can only do straight lines and gentle curves by rotating the fabric as you stitch. And, of course, you can go back and forth by pressing the reverse button occasionally to get a more textured line.
- All stitching will contract the fabric and the quilting stitch will do this more than most because of the tight top tension which is set automatically. If you loosen the top tension then the stitch will not work; if you wish the fabric to stay flat, you will need to have a very strong backing on the fabric. Try using layers of fabric bonded together, which will stiffen them. The alternative is to be positive about the distortion and make use of it to give texture. You may need to loosen the bottom tension slightly when working with layers of fabric or a heavyweight material.

Opposite above: Quilting stitch worked over printed and applied triangles on a painted fabric. The central strip, stitched with black thread, loses the broken line.

Quilting stitch is useful for layering fabrics, for altering the handle of a fabric and giving it more body, and for appliqué. It also makes fantastic backgrounds for adding decorative stitching.

Opposite below: Quilting stitch worked to secure folded scraps of organza. (Sandra Coleridge)

This section of the book introduced some new ideas and revisited old favourites. Do remember to refer back and use some of these as you work through the next two sections.

part two

dissolve
– washing
away

This section of the book deals with water-soluble materials. It covers the films, fabrics and papers that dissolve readily in water, leaving the stitching behind. It is possible to achieve a variety of effects, from light and lacy to heavy and crunchy textures. Motifs stitched on water-soluble fabric can be outlined with cords, applied to background fabrics or joined with further stitch to form borders or complete embroideries. Remember to apply the stitching ideas and techniques from the earlier 'Stitch' section.

Materials and Methods

A considerable choice of materials is available: film in various weights, opaque fabrics or paper. There are many different trade names for the same product. They all work well for their main purpose – supporting stitching and washing away completely. Many of them can be used as stabilizers to support fine fabrics while stitching and then washed away afterwards. The main groups and their purposes are described below; some of the trade names are given in brackets.

Cold Water-soluble Films

These are clear films which come in various weights from fine and flimsy to very thick. The lighter ones can be useful to place over collage embroideries – those where a variety of fabric and yarns are laid over a background – to keep them stable while stitching. However, you may need two layers of the thinner ones (Avalon) for normal stitching. Medium-weight films (Giuliette, Aquafilm) are good for framing-up and using with machine embroidery. There is also a heavy-weight film (Romeo) that can be stitched without a hoop and is good for techniques where some of the film remains to stiffen the embroidery.

Cold Water-soluble Fabrics

Opaque fabric-like solubles (Solufleece, Aquasol, Solusheet) are excellent because the design can be easily seen when drawn and they are strong enough to use with embroidery machines or heavy stitching. These fabrics work best when used in a frame. A recent addition to the range (Bond) is one that is coated with soluble glue, providing a sticky surface that is great for arranging snippets of fabric, silk or wool tops, etc.

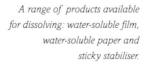

A range of products available for dissolving: water-soluble film, water-soluble paper and sticky stabiliser.

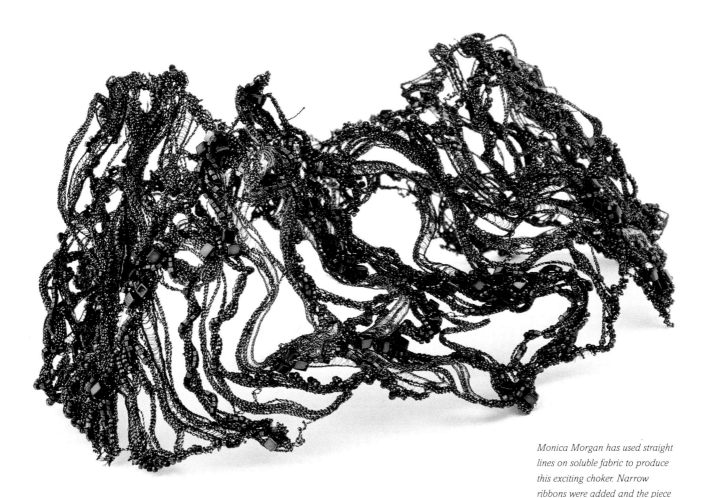

Monica Morgan has used straight lines on soluble fabric to produce this exciting choker. Narrow ribbons were added and the piece was heavily beaded before dissolving. Page 46: Detail of choker.

Cold Water-soluble Paper

This looks like a large sheet of ordinary paper (mark it as soluble when you buy it in case it gets into your paper drawer) but it will dissolve away completely when water is applied. It is very good as a stabilizer for chiffon or other very fine fabrics as it will disappear completely. Although not the best choice as a support for normal machine embroidery, it has a special usefulness in that a resist, such as nail varnish, can be applied; this will prevent areas from washing away. Embroiderers can use this to their advantage, particularly when a design is printed or drawn on it.

Hot Water-soluble Fabric

This organza-like fabric usually needs to be boiled to dissolve, which is something of a disadvantage. However, it has some properties that may be useful. There is usually a shrinkage of the stitching, which can be attractive, and it produces a very soft finished piece.

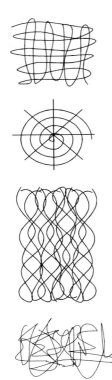

Some grid patterns showing a range of overlapping stitching so that it holds together when the fabric is dissolved.

A page from a notebook showing the use of automatic patterns stitched in overlapping rows to make delicate bands of stitchery. The samples are shown before and after dissolving.

Stitching the Dissolvable Medium

Whichever form of dissolvable medium is used, there are a few rules governing the way it is stitched. Think about the following, remembering that the bobbin thread will show as much as the top thread:

- The stitches, particularly zigzag machine stitches, need to be 'locked' to prevent them from unravelling when the support material is washed away. The best way of doing this is to ensure that all areas are stitched twice. Just work straight stitching over the top and this will do the trick. A grid or mesh, stitched first, will also work to fix the stitches.
- Although straight stitch, with the foot on, will not usually unravel, the patterned stitches may do so, but lines of straight stitch, worked over them, will usually be enough to hold them together. If you want to retain the look of the stitch then work them on top of a grid.
- Remember to join any isolated parts of the design. Any areas not linked to the main stitching will fall away when the support is lost.
- If you are using film and it tears, it is easy to place another piece of film as a patch and carry on stitching. This is useful if you have tension problems which cause a 'bird's nest' under the work.
- If you have patterns – particularly satin stitch patterns – built into your machine, you have access to some good sources of texture for water-soluble stitching. You may, however, have some difficulty stitching automatic patterns, particularly on thick film. Try using a roller foot and make sure that the patterns are not too dense. Make samples of the stitching on small pieces of water-soluble fabric to see how they work when dissolved. Use a larger stitch size and possibly a looser tension when stitching, especially on the film.

Don't worry too much if the fabric puckers as you stitch. This effect will be lost when the fabric is dissolved. Sometimes a certain amount of unravelling of stitches is attractive and may be intentional.

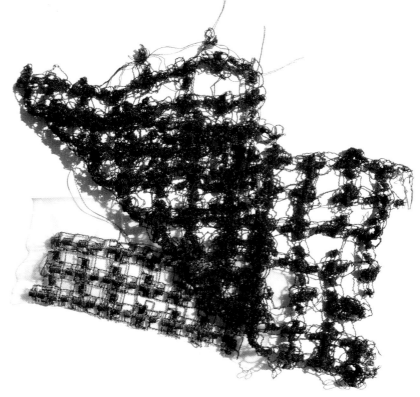

An open fabric made by the same method, showing the dissolved fabric on top.

Dissolving Cold Water-soluble Fabric

When all stitching is complete, cut away any excess film. These fragments can be dampened and laid on non-stick baking paper, overlapping the edges. When dry, it can be re-used. Now work as follows:

1. Pin out the work to be dissolved on a polystyrene tray. Pizza trays are good for this but any base that is waterproof will serve. Remember to place the pins in an area that won't be dissolved away.
2. Although it is known as cold water-soluble, the heavy film will dissolve more quickly in warm water. It does take a while to do so completely, so try leaving it to soak, changing the water.

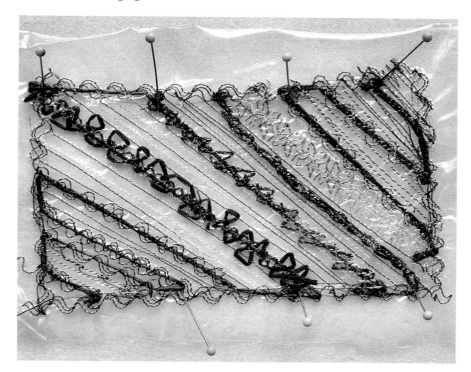

Here you can see the lines of stitch pinned out ready for dissolving. Take care to pin into the stitching and not the film.

3. When dissolving is complete, the embroidery will be floppy. If the piece of work needs shaping, don't dissolve all the material away, and stop rinsing at the jelly stage. Wrap it around a shape for vessels and bowls. Make shapes around pencils for beads and tassels. Allow the piece to dry thoroughly before doing any further work or framing.

Dissolving Hot Water-soluble Fabric

Hot water-soluble fabric is best boiled, as tap water is not usually hot enough. If you want to encourage shrinking, just drop into a pan of gently bubbling water for a few moments. Then, with care and using tongs, plunge it into cold water. To prevent shrinkage (and if the pan size allows), try pinning on polystyrene before 'cooking'.

Embroidery machines are becoming more popular and their requirement for stabilizers has resulted in the development of many of the soluble fabrics we use in this book. New materials are arriving all the time, so keep looking.

Wash-Away Film and Fabric

Techniques for Water-soluble Fabrics

Now that we have covered the basics, we can explore some exciting ways to use the materials. The methods here range from grids and lines of stitch to heavy stitching using machine embroidery techniques. Do refer back to the 'Stitch' section and don't be afraid to experiment.

Diagrams of the stages of stitching used on the piece opposite (top) and front cover. The top diagram shows the straight stitching, the centre one has lines of automatic patterns added, and the final one shows the edging using different automatic patterns.

Straight Lines and Grids

In the earlier section, 'Stitch', we considered grids and strips for their design possibilities. They work very well with water-solubles too. Fine lines of stitching on dissolvable fabric can be very effective, especially when embellished with hand stitch and beads. Try the following.

1. Using Romeo, or one of the muslin-like solubles, draw a rectangle about 15 x 10 cm (6 x 4 in) on your film. With the sewing machine set up for normal stitching (normal sewing foot on and feed dogs up), stitch straight lines on the diagonal as shown in the diagram (left). Vary the space between the lines, stitching some close together. Do plenty of stitching – this technique needs lots of lines. If you have a coverlock machine, as discussed in the 'Stitch' section, the massed lines can be stitched more quickly.

Detail of front cover image, showing the effect of the dripped embossing powder technique.

2. Change to a pattern stitch. If you have satin stitch patterns, you could use one of those. Alternatively, if you only have utility stitches on your machine, try the one that looks like feather stitch. Add some diagonal lines of pattern and then stitch around the outside of the rectangle, over the straight line of stitches, making sure that they are well secured. Remember the thick and thin lines; change the weight of the thread or put two threads through the needle.

3. After stitching but before dissolving, try some of these alternatives:

• Hand stitch over the lines of machining, catching several lines together using buttonhole stitch.
• Lay a heavier thread or yarn next to the line of stitching and use any sort of couching stitch.
• Add beads, cords or wires, stitching them to the straight lines.
• Make beaded chains and couch these over the stitching lines.

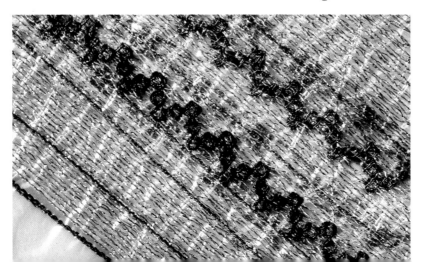

Lines of straight stitching on Romeo film are interspersed with pattern stitches. This will need a row or two of stitch, worked the other way, before dissolving.

   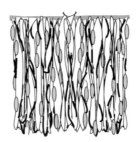 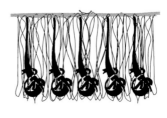

Some ideas for fringes stitched on water-soluble fabric: using straight stitching; with scraps of fabrics included; using previously stitched motifs.

When you have finished embellishing your piece of work, pin it carefully to a suitable surface to dissolve. If you have used a heavy film like Romeo, you may need to soak it for a little while to dissolve the film fully.

After stitching, you could heat embossing powder (Ultra Thick Embossing Enamel – UTEE) in a Melting Pot or a ladle. Heat the UTEE in the ladle from below, using a heat tool. Drip this onto the grid from a height so that it cools as it falls, to make bead-like blobs on the stitching. You could also use wire or wrapped pipe-cleaners to form three-dimensional articles such as jewellery.

other ways to use the grid
- Try making several rectangles and join them for chokers.
- Further embellishments, perhaps also stitched onto water-soluble film, could be used as 'danglies' for the bottom of a choker.
- A fringe could be made from straight lines of stitching on water-soluble film with beads and beaded chains added to them before dissolving, as described in step 3 on page 53.

Fringes

This bracelet was made by stitching straight lines and pattern stitches on Romeo film. Beaded chains and machine-wrapped cords were stitched on to the film before dissolving. Some of the straight lines were left to create the fringed edge.

Think of the possibilities of stitching the straight lines to form a fringe and adding little bursts of satin stitch part way down the line. These could be structured, for example a horizontal burst of stitching on a vertical line, or they could be gradually increasing bands of satin stitch, forming a narrow ogee shape. However, lines of automatic stitching at the top would secure the fringe and, when dissolved, it could be stitched to the bottom of the choker.

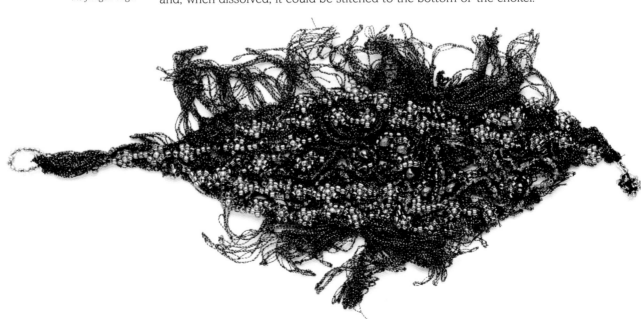

This delicious little bag shows how effective a fringe can be. The body of the bag was laid on water-soluble film and the edges and fringes were then stitched over it. (Carol Coleman)

Finger knitting is a technique that you usually learn before you are old enough to use knitting needles (look on the internet if you need instructions). Use fine or delicate knitting ribbons or thicker hand or machine threads. These are better than knitting yarns for this purpose. Work a short length and remove from your fingers. Pin out onto heavy water-soluble film, pushing and pulling to distort it. Then stitch, either freehand or with a built-in pattern, working out and beyond the edge to make a fringe.

A water-soluble edging for a ribbon, knitting ribbon or flat braid can then be used as a fringe, looping it along a fabric edge. Pin the ribbon to Romeo film and work back and forth diagonally across it, stitching a small, tight circle on each edge of the ribbon. Dissolve and use as required.

Right: The diagrams show ways of stitching pieces of finger knitting to secure it and add extra fringing on the edges.

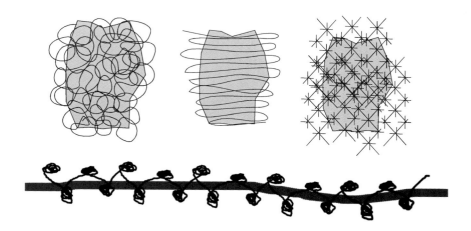

Right: Diagram of stitching on a knitting tape or narrow ribbon to make a picot braid.

Knitting tape was wrapped around straws and the picot braid looped back and forth to add texture and to make a fringe.

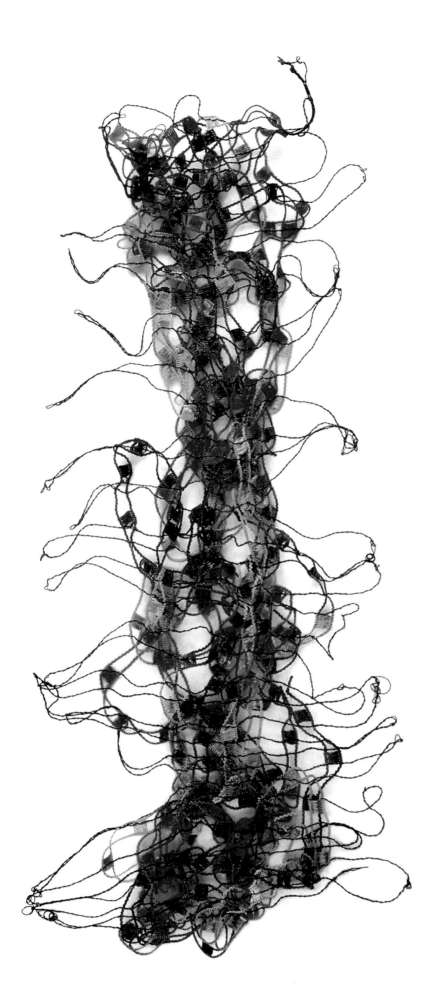

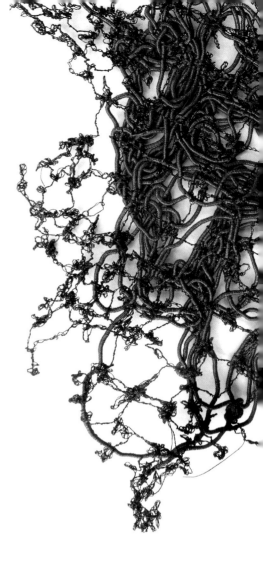

Finger knitting using gimp, laid on water-soluble film and then stitched over with an automatic pattern in a grid.

Finger knitting using a delicate knitting tape, then stitched over on water-soluble film using free stitchery.

Using Motifs with Water-soluble Film

So far, we have concentrated on using straight lines or grids with wash-away media. Bringing in small design components as motifs extends the use of soluble material and brings an element of design into the work.

Shapes or motifs can be cut from a fabric, or a previously stitched motif could be used. Fabric can be bonded to felt and then shapes cut from it. The shapes could then be laid on the water-soluble medium and lacy edges stitched. They could also be joined to form strips which are then woven or stitched to a background. Use the grids and strips described on page 50 for ideas. Geometric shapes would work well here.

Lay the cut shapes on the water-soluble film and stitch straight lines, continuing the stitch over the fabric shapes. It may look fine like this or you may need to do more stitching around the edges of the motifs or to add detail to them.

A finished folded book that has used the design motifs from the opposite page. The stitched pieces have been applied over dyed Tissuetex on felt.

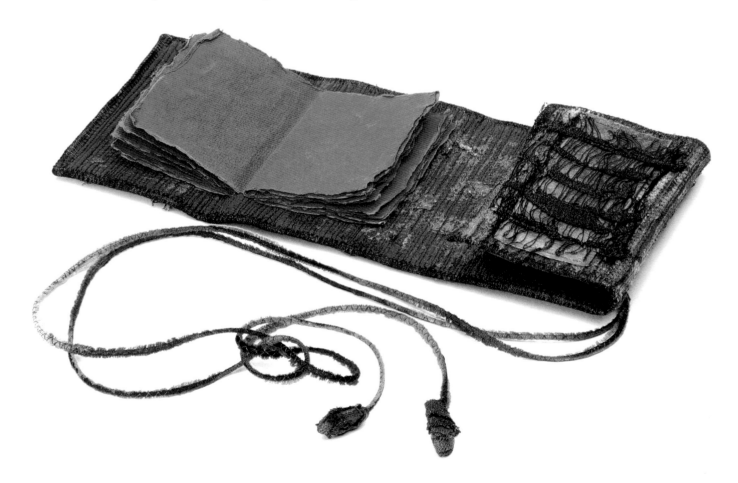

Above: A photograph of a plastic toy for a bird cage. It was scanned in to create the black images above left. This design was then scanned into the sewing machine and digitised.

Left: An Art Nouveau motif that has been scanned into the sewing machine and digitised. The motif has been used with stitching on waster dissolvable fabric, shown here both before and after dissolving.

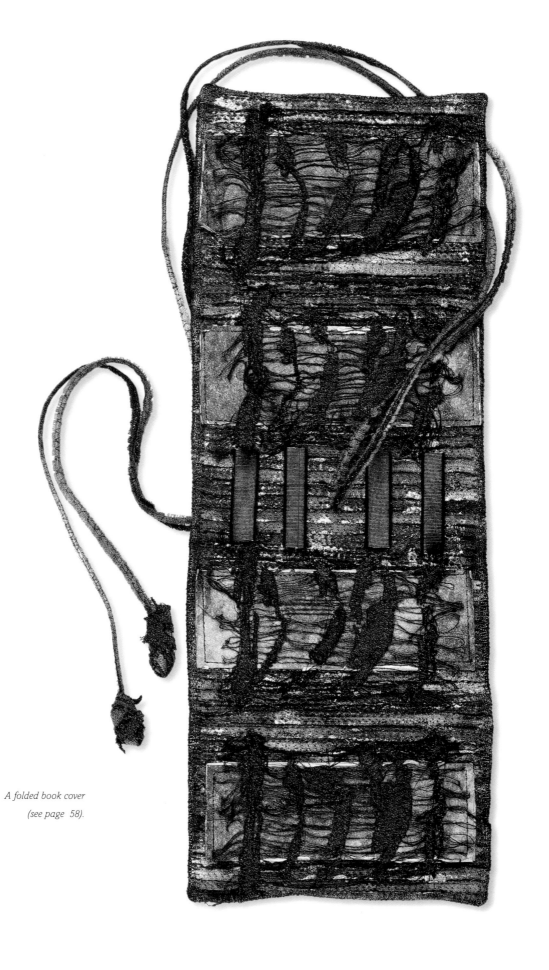

A folded book cover
(see page 58).

Filling in Drawn Shapes

A slightly different effect can be obtained by drawing the shape onto the film and filling in the outline with solid stitching. These filled areas could then be overstitched with the straight lines to provide a contrast.

- Look for a simple shape: one that you can draw or trace from a suitable pattern book (watch out for copyright), or use a foam or rubber stamp.
- Draw (using a permanent pen in a colour close to your thread) or stamp the design onto the film, using a stamp pad. Bear in mind that the colour may run and affect your stitching. Metallic pads work with most colours. Frame the fabric or film reasonably tightly.
- Set up the sewing machine for machine embroidery by dropping the feed dogs and attaching the darning foot. Now use free-running straight stitch to outline the shape you have drawn.
- Fill in the centre with further solid stitching, perhaps more free-running stitch, working in two directions. Granite stitch (really tiny overlapping circles) would also be a good choice, making sure that it locks with the outline.

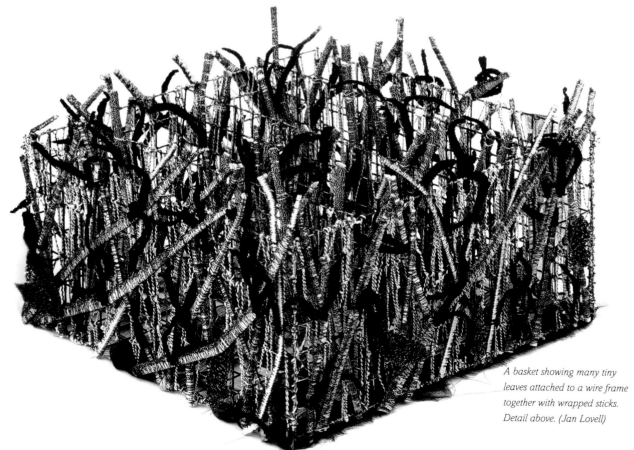

A basket showing many tiny leaves attached to a wire frame together with wrapped sticks. Detail above. (Jan Lovell)

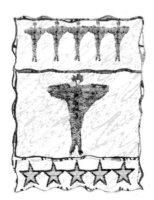

These shapes or motifs can be put together into borders. Consider geometric shapes such as triangles, ogees or circles. Alternatively, flowers, leaf shapes or ethnic motifs could be used but be careful to make sure that they are not too fussy to stitch.

The good thing about working on water-soluble fabric is that all the pieces can be made as slips or small completed sections of embroidery and then arranged and rearranged to make a pleasing border or complete piece of work.

These 'slips' can be applied separately to a previously stitched background, such as leaves on a tree. Or they could be placed on another piece of water-soluble fabric, but pay attention to the shapes formed at the point where the motifs meet – the negative spaces. These should be at least as interesting as the positive ones. Use extra stitching to join them. This joining stitch may be worked in a random way to be unobtrusive or could be stitched in circles, lines or small squares to make a further pattern.

These slips could also be solid embroidery on fabrics. The joining stitches on water-soluble fabric act as insertion stitches and provide a contrast of texture.

Outlining Motifs with Cords

A further technique that brings in the use of motifs is to make machine-wrapped cords to outline areas of motifs that have been previously stitched on water-soluble film. Choose a design that isn't fussy. You are going to have to couch cords around most of your design so it shouldn't be very intricate. Draw this design onto the water-soluble film, tracing from your source material, and shade in the areas to be filled with stitching and outlined with cord. This will help when you come to stitch it. Now frame up the film, ready for stitching.

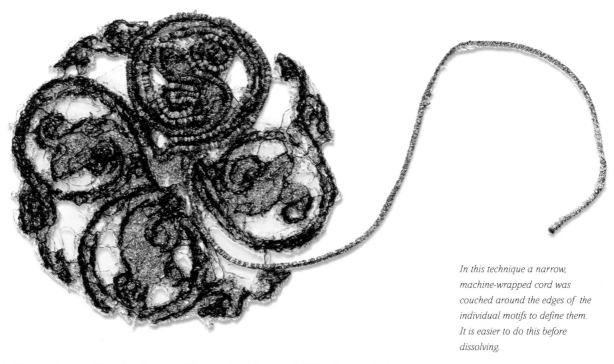

In this technique a narrow, machine-wrapped cord was couched around the edges of the individual motifs to define them. It is easier to do this before dissolving.

1. Set up the machine for free machine embroidery and fill in the shaded areas, changing the thread colour and using a lacy stitch (the stitch shouldn't be too heavy at this stage) as a filling. Remember that the bobbin thread will be visible and take this into account. Leave some areas free of stitching but make sure that they are joined at some point or they will fall out when dissolved.

2. Cut off any trailing threads and make machine-wrapped cords as follows. Set the machine for free machining and select several quite chunky threads. Lower the presser foot and stitch over the threads using your widest zig zag until they are completely covered. Remember that the bobbin thread will show, so use a suitable colour. Make the cord quite narrow.

Opposite, below: This diagram shows how stamps can provide design elements. The angel stamp, by Sherrill Kahn, is available in two sizes and so could form a main motif, as well as a border. These could be stamped on to the film and stitched, using free running stitch with whip stitch outlines. A star stamp could form the lower border.

3. Now, before dissolving the film, stitch the cord around the selected areas of the motif. Unless your design is very simple, it is easier to couch the cord by hand around the filled areas either using a straightforward oversewing technique or, possibly, a more complex couching stitch to attach it to the water-soluble film.

4. Seal the edges of the cord with a small blob of adhesive or hold it in a candle flame for a second or two. When completed, pin it to a dissolving board and dissolve the film as before.

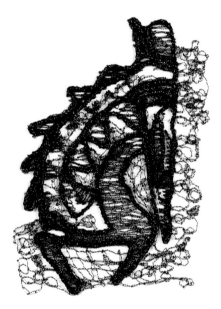

This design was based on an African comb. It was simplified and drawn on Romeo film before free running stitch was worked, very lightly, in the main areas. Before dissolving, the wrapped cords were couched by hand around the shapes. The final effect can be seen in the dissolved piece on the right. This motif is edged with some additional stitching.

Using these Motifs

The stitched motifs could be used to make up larger pieces by stitching a variety of them and joining together, laying them on water-soluble paper as before and stitching all over them to give a lacy effect. Try changing the scale, making some motifs bigger or smaller. Perhaps make a sampler with bands of pattern dividing the motifs. Alternatively, they could be joined to form borders.

Motifs could be applied to a previously painted or textured background, perhaps a velvet with chiffon distressed on top of it, and the pattern could be built up in layers over this background.

Alternative Outlining Technique

- Cut pieces of fabric into some of the shapes of the motif and stitch them to the water-soluble film. Think carefully about placing the pieces so that the design is not unbalanced. Net and lace would be good; the lace can be painted afterwards.
- Make the machine-wrapped cord first and then arrange it into a pattern on the water-soluble film. Pin it in place and draw around it with a ballpoint pen. Then take the cord away and do the stitching following the drawn pattern. Couch the cord on afterwards, as before.
- Lay the cord over the film in a random but pleasing manner. Pin in place. Machine stitch over it with an open pattern or zigzag or utility stitch, removing pins as you go. Make this thread a contrast. Free machine in the areas between the cords.
- Use wrapped pipe-cleaners instead of zigzag cords in the exercise above. Bend them into shapes before pinning.

Sticky Soluble Stabilizers

A fairly new addition to the water-soluble stable of fabrics is a sticky, wash-away stabilizer which makes building up collaged surfaces very easy. You cut the sticky stabilizer to fit the embroidery frame, peel off the backing and place it, sticky side up, on a work surface. Taping down the corners makes it easier. Now build up layers using a variety of fibres: silk tops, ribbons, jazzy yarns, scraps of fabric. They will stick to the surface but can easily be moved. When you are happy with the arrangement, place ordinary water-soluble film on top, making sure that it covers all the sticky bits. Take away the tape, frame up the sandwich and free machine (or use the embroidery unit, if you have one) to stitch your design, making sure that you've stitched over all the trapped material. When you are happy with the stitching, pin it out in the usual way and just wash away the support fabrics.

Give some consideration to the design of the stitching. Random lines may work well but it is usually better to have an idea in mind. You could try the grid structure discussed on page 50. It would be an interesting exercise to lay a grid of fancy yarns on top of the sticky surface. Then try a variety of ways to stitch into the grid. Some of these could be done by:

- Free machining into the yarns, filling the centre of each space with lacy stitching
- Placing a tiny scrap of fabric in the centre of each square, stitching around and over it to secure
- Laying lines of previously dissolved automatic pattern along the lines of the grid and stitching them in.

The stabilizer is on a firm backing and it is possible to print on it using an inkjet printer. It may be safer to attach it first to plain paper as a carrier. Just use a glue stick or double-sided tape around the edges to hold it. This is a good way to transfer designs. It is also robust enough to take a rubber-stamp print.

A wash-away, sticky stabilizer was used to make this embroidery. It was taped to a surface and fine silk fibres added. The fibres were then covered with fine water-soluble film before motifs were stitched over the top. The stabilizer and film were then dissolved to leave a translucent fabric.

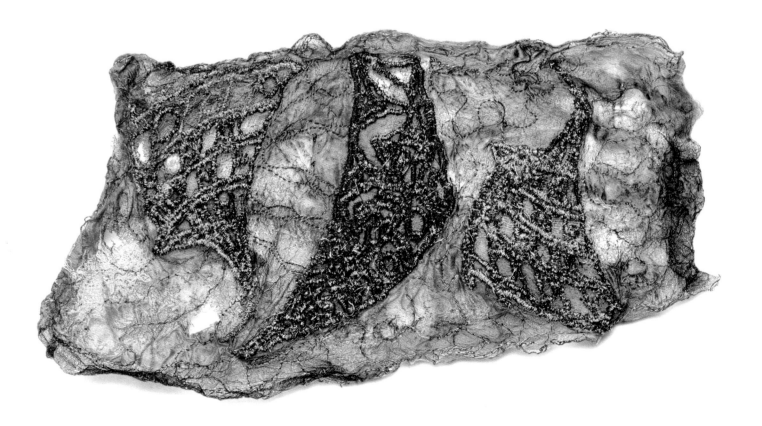

Water-Soluble Paper

Cold water-dissolvable paper (not fabric) is sold as a stabilizer for fine fabrics. It works well used in this way, but it can also be painted with resists, which protect certain areas and prevent them washing away. When combined with stitch, this adds exciting options for embroiderers. It can also be pressed into a block or stamp and wetted to make a very fine cast.

Water-soluble paper is placed on a metal block and wetted to make a pulp. When dry, this can be removed from the block and incorporated into a stitched piece.

Making Paper Casts

Although you can make paper to be used for casting from blocks, it is a messy process and takes some time. Water-soluble paper is quick and easy. The results can be very fine and delicate. Work like this:

1. You will need a wooden block, stamp or similar surface to make the paper cast. The wooden Indian blocks are probably the best, not least because the colour bleeds out into the paper with unpredictable results, which are usually delightful. However, the cheap foam blocks and rubber stamps often work really well. You will also need the paper, water and a medium-size paintbrush.

2. Forming the paper on the block is a simple operation. Just tear pieces of paper, lay them on top of the block and dampen with a paintbrush. Cover the block, not too heavily, and then continue to add water until the surface has become pulp. Now use the brush, or your finger, to move the pulp around so that you have thick and thin surfaces. If the block is deeply inscribed, as some foam blocks are, be sure to push plenty of pulp into the gaps. The paper should be gooey at this stage, not looking like paper at all. Clear a few areas of pulp to give some holes for a distressed effect. There will probably be more paper over the thin areas than necessary, so push it away quite ruthlessly. It may look as though there's no paper left, but it will be there.

Right: The paper cast (shown on the previous page) has been coloured and stitched into a background made from velvet and chiffon. It has then been free machined and distressed with a heat tool.

3. Dab off excess water with a kitchen towel, taking care not to remove the pulp. The paper will take quite a time to dry. Leave it overnight in an airing (warm) cupboard or close to the central heating boiler or hot water tank. If it is sunny, placing it in the car is very good too. I find it best to use only a part of the block or stamp as this results in a delicate fragmented effect. Small scraps of stitching, previously worked on water-soluble film and dissolved, can be laid over the block before the paper is pressed into it.

Colouring casts

The casts can be coloured at the pulp stage by dropping runny paints, inks or watered-down acrylics onto the pulp while it is wet. This results in pastel colours, which can be very attractive. Strong tea, coffee or walnut ink work well at the wet stage too. Just drip the colour from a brush or use a pipette.

If a stronger colour is needed, wait until the paper is dry. Tease it away from the block very gently, using the tip of a craft knife to lift reluctant areas. Don't worry if it tears a little – that will add to the aged effect.

- Use acrylic paints at this stage as very wet paint could turn it back into pulp. With a medium-size, soft paintbrush, push the paint well into the paper until no white gaps are seen.
- Blend two or three colours together, merging them into each other.
- Don't worry if it all seems rather flat – just rub on a little metallic wax which will really bring out the detail. Powders such as PearlEx can be brushed on after the wax, which will hold them on the paper.

Apply the paper cast to a prepared background and hand or machine stitch to add detail.

Using Resists with Water-soluble Paper

Water-soluble paper washes away very easily and this feature can be exploited by protecting some areas with a resist. Here is the basic method.

1. The design can be drawn with coloured pencils, computer printed or stamped onto the paper. You could also use an outline design and paint it later. Don't use water-colours (or any medium that is wet) or it will dissolve. Acrylic paint won't wash away; this can be an advantage and we will cover that later. Try scanning some basic sketchbook motifs or a digital photograph, perhaps enhancing them by using special effects in your paint program to swirl or distort them.

2. When printed, stitch some areas of the motif using either free machine techniques or straight lines of stitching. The lines may not show on the final result but they hold it all together. Most machines stitch quite happily on this paper but, if you have any trouble, try using the paper double or backed with water-soluble fabric. Be particularly careful when moving to another area of the paper. Don't pull. Just lift the presser foot and ease away gently.

Jan Hay took a digital photograph of some colourful leaves (above) and used it for this series of work on water-soluble paper (below left). The digital photograph was printed on water-soluble paper and stitched with straight lines to give stability. The areas to be retained were painted with clear nail polish and the remainder washed away.

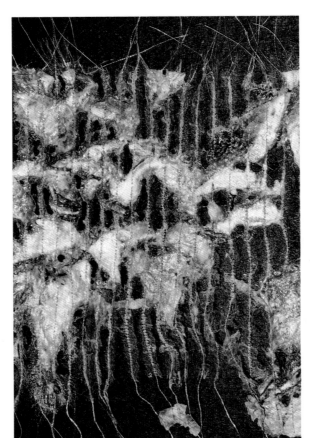

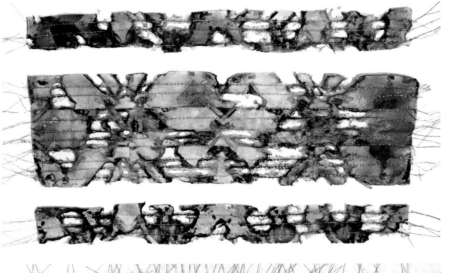

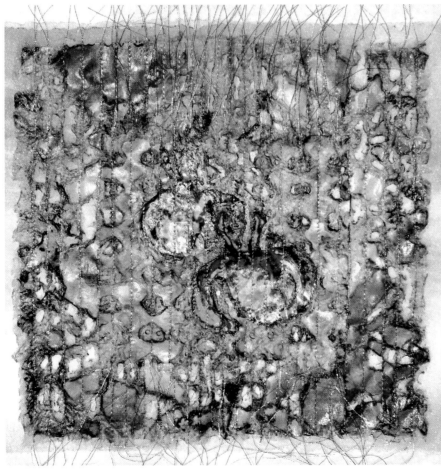

Opposite page right: The photograph was then used as a base for a computer design. Here you can see it part way through the dissolving process. (Jan Hay)

Left: The three elements of the design shown on the opposite page demonstrate the effectiveness of the resist and dissolve technique. (Jan Hay)

A further photograph of water lilies was printed, resisted and combined with the previous pieces for a delicate final textile. The threads from the initial stitching add to the ethereal effect. (Jan Hay)

3. Areas of the design, those not to be dissolved away, are then painted with clear nail polish or PVA (white) glue on a fine brush. Other resists to try could be Markal oil-bars (try a rubbing) or metallic paints. Do not paint it on too heavily or you won't achieve the crumbly distressed look. It will look pretty odd at this stage.

4. The machined, painted paper is then firmly pinned to a piece of foam, polystyrene or similar waterproof material, making sure that the pins are in the painted areas. A wet paintbrush is then used to dissolve the unwanted parts. Some areas may need encouragement with a little gentle finger rubbing. Dab gently with kitchen paper and dry in a warm place or with a hair-dryer. It takes a long time to dry and may be best in your airing (warm) cupboard overnight.

5. If the design was an outline only, perhaps an individual motif, you can paint it with acrylics and, when dry, enhance the surface with Treasure Gold, metallic wax or a similar product. Alternatively, use Stampers' Embossing Ink and Powder sparingly and heat with a 'Heat-It' craft tool. Mix the colours of the embossing powders for special effects.

The paper pieces are quite strong, in spite of their delicate appearance, and can be applied to backgrounds or made into jewellery. It is usually best to hand-stitch motifs to backgrounds. Try combining the finished paper piece with some strips of pattern, stitched on water-soluble film and dissolved.

Extensions

Another way of making motifs with water-soluble paper is to use stamps (the foam ones are best) or stencils. Brush the stamp, or sponge through the stencil, with PVA glue or acrylic paint. Allow to dry, stitch and then wash away the paper between the motifs, as before.

A further method is to stitch rows of automatic pattern on the paper and then paint, resist and dissolve. For a delicate filigree effect, stitch some of the machine's automatic cross-stitch patterns on the paper. Do not use resist, just brush with the paintbrush and water. Even without a resist, the paper will cling around the stitching. This produces lovely lacy pieces which can be gilded with embossing powder for an enchanting effect when merged with other pieces of stitching.

Left: A rubber stamp of leaves was printed on water-soluble paper with a standard inkpad and drawn into with coloured pencils, blending the colours together. White gesso was dabbed on with a sponge. Painting the leaves with nail polish resist preserved them when water was used to wash away parts of the design.

Below: The leaf design (see left) partly dissolved. The gesso does not need to be resisted and gives a good contrast of textures.

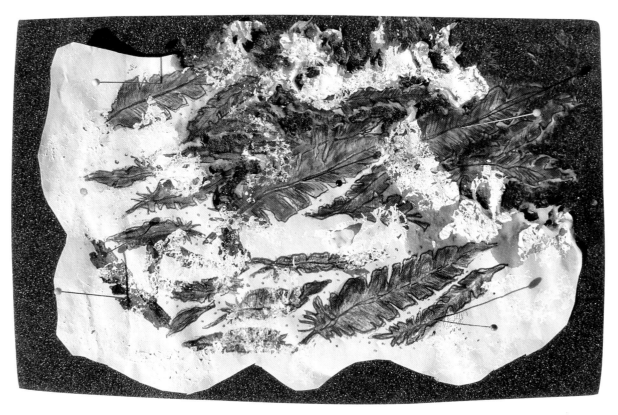

Water-soluble Paper with Puff Paint

Try these ideas:

- Use puff paint on the paper. Stamp or sponge and then stitch and dissolve, as before, and allow to dry.
- Alternatively, stitch first, and partially or totally dissolve the paper, then sponge or paint the puff paint on and dry.
- You could also place the paper over a wire grid and dissolve so that the paper clings to the wire when dissolved. Back this with a stitched piece and work further hand stitches into it.

Right: Water-soluble paper between two layers of net have been stitched with an automatic pattern.

The sandwich shown was partially dissolved and painted with puff paint when dry. It was cut into strips and woven through stitched wire mesh and decorated with scraps of stitching worked on water-soluble film.

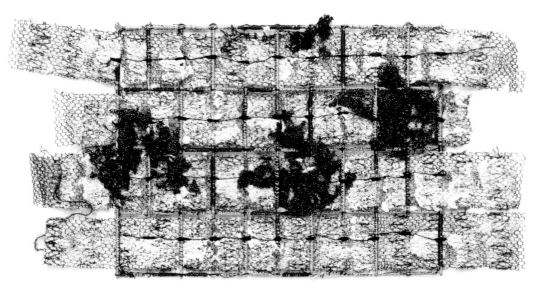

Kozo Fibres and Water-soluble Paper

Kozo fibres are used by paper makers. They are chopped into a paper pulp or soaked, shredded and liquidized to make the paper. The fibres combine well with water-soluble paper to produce a strong paper-like background with an intriguing surface texture. Any similar fibre will work in the same way.

1. Soak the Kozo fibres for one hour, then cut or tease apart. Paint if required and allow to dry.

2. Lay out a piece of water-soluble paper and place some teased-out fibres over it. Then place another piece of paper on top, making a sandwich. Dissolve with a brush, pushing the paper around and revealing the fibres. When dry, paint with acrylics and gild with metallic paints or wax. The results can be backed with fabric and could have hand or machine stitches added.

Kozo fibres were placed on water-soluble paper. Another piece of the paper was then stamped, resisted with embossing powder and laid over the fibres. Water was used to wash away some of the paper, prior to colouring with Adirondack colour wash sprays.

Try the following ideas:

- Lay out the paper and stamp a pattern in the centre of it. Now free machine, following the pattern of the stamp. Make a border top and bottom from the fibres. Pin to a support and use a brush to remove paper. Dry, paint and gild.

Above: Water-soluble paper with lines of straight stitching was combined with Kozo fibres. It was then stamped with a large foam stamp. The stamps were sprinkled with embossing powder, which resisted the water when washing away.

Water-soluble paper and Kozo fibres. While the paper was damp a cast paper stamp was embedded in the pulp. When dry it was painted with acrylic paints and lightly waxed with metallic wax.

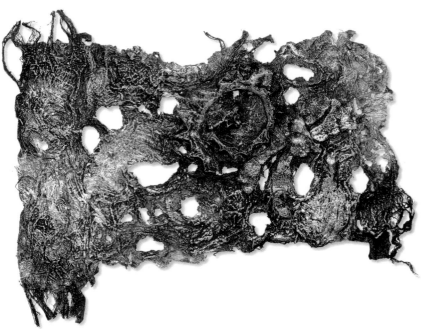

- Make a paper sandwich with the Kozo in the middle, as before. Stamp with a large foam stamp using embossing ink. Sprinkle with embossing powder and heat to activate it. Stitch and dissolve as before, working through to the Kozo layer. The embossing powder will act as a resist, preserving the stamped area.

- Paint Kozo and tease into shapes such as trees, leaves or abstract shapes. Dry and paint. Stitch to water-soluble fabric, such as Romeo or Solusheet, making sure that the Kozo is well stitched to the background. Add other scraps and braids and define shapes with wrapped cords. Dissolve.

This atmospheric landscape panel incorporates fabrics treated with painted Bondaweb (fusible webbing), free machine stitching and pieces of water-soluble stitching. Kozo fibres give added texture. (Monica Morgan)

Scrubbed Paper Napkins

This process also uses paper and washes it away but, instead of purpose-made water-soluble paper, it works with easily obtainable materials: photocopy paper, two layers of tissue, paper napkins, newspaper or similar papers. We have covered the technique in previous books but have since discovered the joys of working with the colourful paper napkins that are available today. The papers are stitched using a grid of straight stitching before being scrubbed and washed away to leave an attractive distressed effect. They can be coloured before or after stitching.

Here is the basic process.

1. If possible, paint the paper first using permanent paints that won't dissolve in water. Silk paints or sprays like the Tagger or Adirondack colour washes work well. Acrylics may hinder the dissolving action. If paper napkins have a good colour, they can be left. The designs can be an asset and can be incorporated in the work. The paper can easily be painted afterwards so don't worry too much about this stage.

Left: Diagram of a grid stitched on a painted paper napkin.

Right: A patterned paper napkin was first stitched with a grid and then around the pattern.

2. Stitch a grid using the edge of the presser foot as a guide. Just line up each row by setting the edge of the foot against the previous row. The grid can be straight or diagonal. Don't worry if the paper crumples.

3. If you are using a paper napkin, free machine around the pattern as well as adding the lines to make a grid. The napkin will certainly crumple and this contributes to the texture.

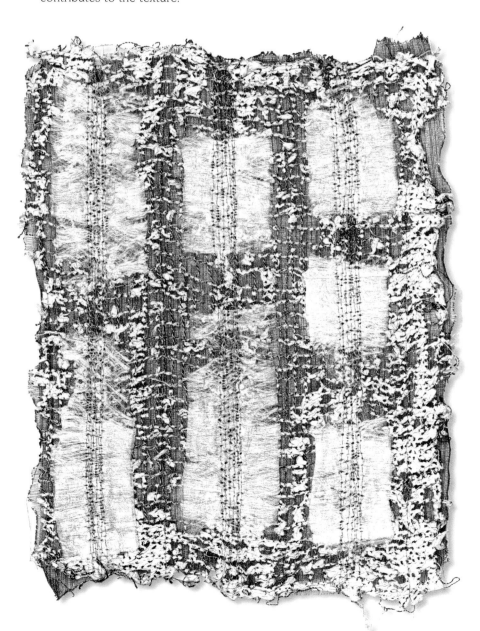

Split silk carrier rods were stitched to a fine paper grid with lines of gold thread and then scrubbed. This was laid over striped silk organza and stitched again to secure.

4. When the stitching is complete, hold the piece under the tap to get very wet and then scrub (washerwoman style) to lose some of the paper. Do this over a bowl and dispose of the water in the garden.

5. Spread it out to dry and add further painting in a dabbing motion if it needs it.

A finished paper napkin grid was placed between two layers of fine chiffon scarf, together with some wisps of blue fibres, and stitched to secure. The chiffon was then partially melted with a heat gun.

There are lots of ways to use the grids. You could place them on a background fabric and add further stitching, manipulate by folding or scrunching and then place between water-soluble film and stitch. Try with a narrow grid or vary the grid lines to change the scale. There are lots of possibilities and you will want to add more of your own.

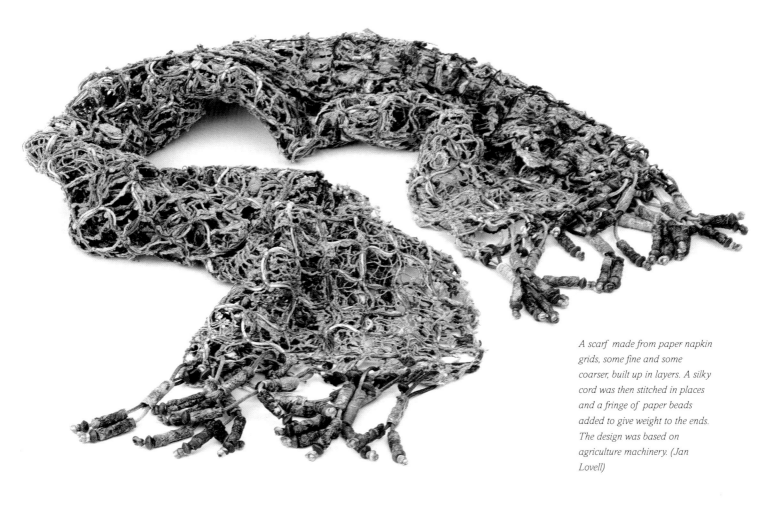

A scarf made from paper napkin grids, some fine and some coarser, built up in layers. A silky cord was then stitched in places and a fringe of paper beads added to give weight to the ends. The design was based on agriculture machinery. (Jan Lovell)

Combining the Media

Handmade Paper and Water-soluble Film

Interesting effects can be obtained by working with paper-making techniques and strips of dissolved water-soluble patterns. Stitch lines of automatic pattern on water-soluble film and dissolve it. Now prepare and liquidize paper linters, plant material or paper pulp into a liquid state (do consult a book specifically on paper-making if necessary) and form into squares on a damp kitchen cloth (couching cloth). Just dribble the pulp into rough squares. Lay the dissolved water-soluble grid over the squares, pushing them into the pulp to ensure that they are firmly fixed.

You could also try wetting purchased papers to soften them before embedding the dissolved stitching into them. Set the paper shapes into the grid.

When dry, paint with acrylics or water-colours, depending on the effect required.

Try both of these methods with diagonal and asymmetric grids.

Strips of machine-made lace on water-soluble film were embedded in squares of coloured hand-made paper.

Water-soluble Film and Water-soluble Paper

Interesting combinations can be put together using all forms of water-soluble media. Revisiting the grid structures created at the beginning of this section (page 50) can be rewarding.

Method 1

1. Stitch a grid structure on Romeo film and fill in some of the spaces.
2. Dissolve and dry.
3. Make a drip-mould using the Melting Pot or ladle by dripping melted Ultra Thick Embossing Enamel (UTEE) onto a rubber stamp. While it is still hot, press water-soluble paper onto the back of the embossing powder. Take care as it will be hot.
4. Release when cool.
5. Lay the Romeo grid on baking paper. Place the water-soluble paper and embossing powder shape over it. Dampen the paper to make a pulp. Press into the grid. Allow to dry, then paint and wax.

Method 2

1. Work rows of automatic patterns or Flower Stitch circles on Romeo film and dissolve as usual.
2. Stamp water-soluble paper with puff paint and heat to raise the paint. Lay on baking parchment.
3. Wet with a brush and push the pulp about, setting the stitched Romeo into it. Sprinkle or spray with silk paints to colour.

Think about design: perhaps use puff paint areas as borders and the Romeo stitching as a centrepiece.

This section of the book should have given you ideas for using many different varieties of water-soluble materials. Remember that new techniques sometimes take a time to master and it may be that the design you are using is not quite right. Do keep trying as a little perseverance can bring great delight. Keep the ideas in your mind and consider them as you work through the remainder of the book, as many will combine with other materials and methods described in the 'Distort' section.

Below left: A diamond-shaped grid was machined on water-soluble film, using free running stitch with some of the shapes filled. Water-soluble paper, with drips of embossing powder, was used to fill further diamond shapes within the grid.

Below right: Flower stitched circles on Romeo film were pressed into water-soluble paper at the pulp stage. Silk paints were dripped on while the paper was wet, resulting in a pastel effect.

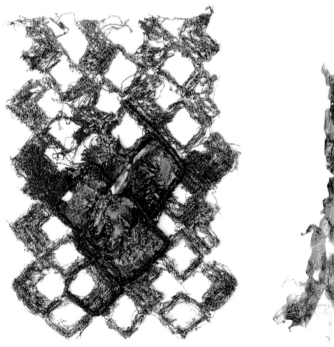
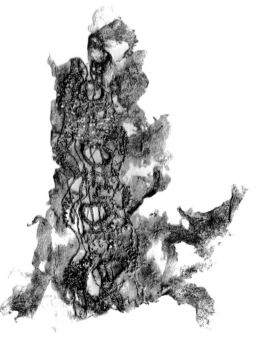

part three

distorting the fabric

This section is about using methods, materials and equipment to change the nature of the fabric or embroidery. Some of the methods are adaptations of traditional techniques and some use new and exciting materials to give effect to the distortion. There are three categories in this section.

- Attacking the Fabric looks at ways to distress, cut, punch or remove threads from the basic fabric, before or after stitching.
- Melting the Fabric is about applying heat by the use of heat tools to texture or melt fabrics. It also covers meltable resources such as embossing powders and puff paints as well as materials like Sizoflor and Thermogauze.
- Shaping the Fabric explains how to use hardening agents, wires and meshes with fabric or stitched pieces. This process gives durability to fragile pieces and adds dramatic shape and undulation.

Materials and Equipment

The materials used in this section range from waste canvas to embossing powders. These materials are described in more depth at the beginning of each subsection. The equipment is also wide ranging, from a needle felt tool to a pot for melting embossing powder. Again, the details of these pieces of equipment are covered throughout this section; see also the list of suppliers on page 126.

Attacking the Fabric

Previous page: Strips of different fabrics were laid on a base of felt and embellished. Further pieces of stitching worked on water-soluble film were added and embellished further (Bev Beattie).

Altering the surface of a fabric can be an excellent way to add texture, distort or even make patterns in a base fabric. The resulting embroideries may form a background for further stitching or may be complete in themselves.

Drawn Thread

Below: Machine drawn thread worked on a curtain fabric. Puff paint was painted to give added texture.

This is a time-honoured hand embroidery method for enhancing fabric. Threads are withdrawn or removed from the fabric, which was traditionally linen with a regular weave. Wrapping and whipping were then worked on the remaining threads, pulling them into bars.

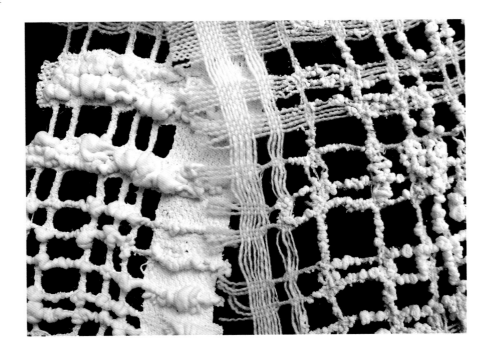

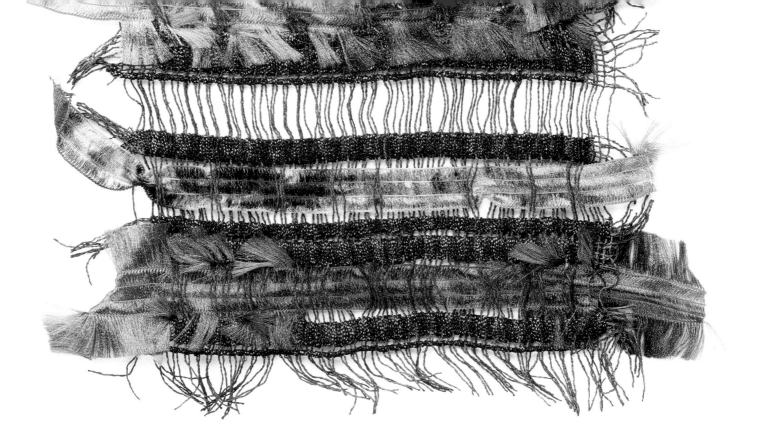

This technique from the past can be brought up to date with unusual fabrics such as openweave curtain fabric, hessian, scrim or waste canvas; all these can be stitched and combined with other media to provide texture and colour.

Threads withdrawn from painted and stitched waste canvas, which is threaded with knitting tapes.

Pull the threads from the fabric, isolating each thread with a pin and pulling out. Remove a few threads to make a gap. These gaps can be in one or both directions. Then use the zigzag stitch, dropping the teeth, with a darning or free embroidery foot to pull groups of threads together. This technique can be used to produce an open grid fabric which can be painted or embellished with embossing powders or puff paint.

Waste Canvas

Waste canvas is intended for working counted thread techniques on unsuitable fabrics such as felt. The idea is to lay the waste canvas over the top and work the counted thread stitches over both fabrics. Because the canvas is held together with a soluble glue, it can be unstuck by damping or spraying with water. This leaves the threads loose and they can then be removed so that just the stitches remain. Used alone, this is an exciting material for machine embroidery, allowing stitches to be built up and fabric strips, ribbons or yarns to be woven through. It can be painted first (silk paints are best), or the whole piece can be coloured afterwards. The best size to use is 10 (double) threads per inch; higher thread counts make it much more difficult to remove the threads.

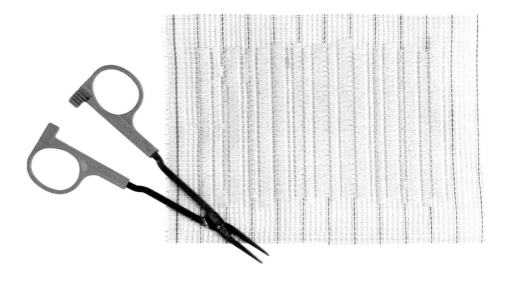

Satin stitching on waste canvas before the threads were pulled out. Electrical forceps make light work of withdrawing the threads.

Ways of stitching waste canvas to give different patterns.

The basic technique is worked like this:

1. Paint the canvas and heat-set the paints if necessary. Alternatively, leave unpainted and work in white threads so that it can all be painted after stitching.

2. Start by working across the canvas using the widest zigzag that you have. Close the zigzag to give a solid satin stitch and remember not to start too near the edge or you won't be able to form a fringe when it is frayed. Work in bands or bars of stitching.

3. When all is stitched, run the piece under warm water. It should go limp and the threads will then be easy to withdraw. Use your fingers or scissors to withdraw the threads, holding the stitching as you pull. For intricate designs, use artery (from scissors suppliers) or electrical forceps (from electronic components suppliers).

4. Having pulled out all the threads you can, if desired, paint with silk or fabric paints.

Some possible variations:

- Thread ribbons, yarns etc. through the gaps between the rows of stitching.
- Twist the work into a shape when it is wet, or coat with a hardener (see page 120). This can be done on a whole piece or with narrow strips.
- Lay the waste canvas over another fabric, such as lace or organza, stitching through both layers and withdrawing the threads, as usual. When it is dry it can be distorted with a heat gun.
- Apply the finished piece to a background fabric. An embellished surface would show up the loops and threads well.

Stitched waste canvas with threads pulled out in one direction.

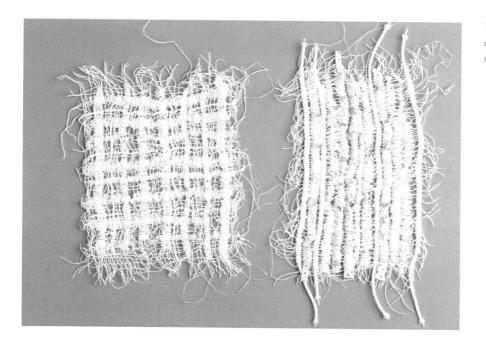

Waste canvas stitched in both directions with threads pulled out in both directions.

Pulled Work

In this technique the stitching pulls the threads of the fabric together, creating holes or gaps. It is best to use a loose weave: scrim or sinamay, a natural fibre often used in millinery. When new, sinamay is very stiff and doesn't pull easily; as it ages, it becomes softer. To soften, rub well between the hands for some time. You could make your own fabric on water-soluble film.

Use satin stitch to pull the woven fibres together. This will distort the weave of the fabric, leaving gaps. You could also:
- use maxi patterns, if you have them, or meander with the satin stitch, as shown (on opposite page).
- make shapes such as spirals, or work a series of shapes to form an overall pattern.
- work with thread that is the same colour as the fabric and then place the stitched piece on a coloured background.
- dab puff paint, such as Xpandaprint, on the finished piece and heat with a heat gun; the result could be painted.

Pulled work on sinamay (natural fibre often used in millinery), threaded with knitting tapes. Blue fibres were laid on top and secured with the Embellisher.

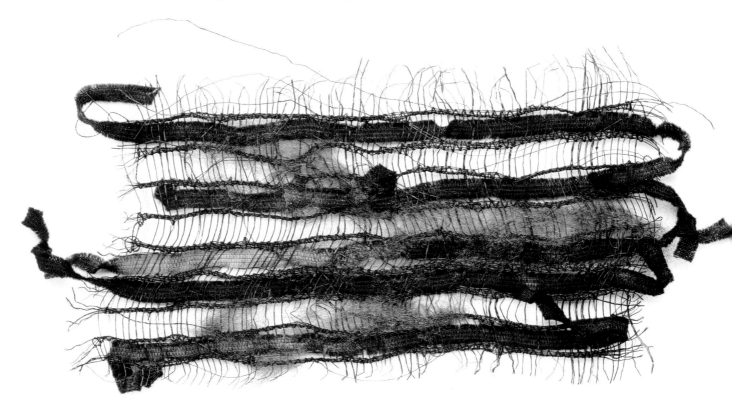

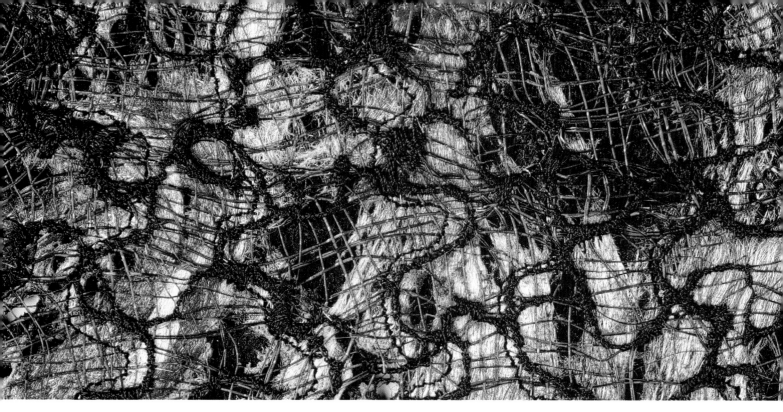

A piece of stitching on sinamay, similar to the central image below, was laid over multi-coloured trilobel nylon and a layer of fabric. It has been stitched freely and then attacked with a heat gun to melt the fibres.

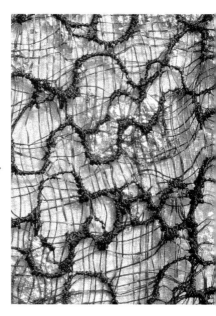

An automatic pattern stitched on felt.

The same automatic pattern stitched on sinamay.

The same stitched sinamay piece laid over pink chiffon with gold leaf embedded.

Using Dry Felting Tools and Techniques

Dry felting techniques have, by their very name, been used exclusively for felting. However, both the hand tools and the Embellisher machine can be invaluable in producing a textured or distressed surface on fabrics such as chiffon or organza.

Hand Tools

It is possible to buy individual barbed needles for dry felting but it is much quicker to invest in a hand needle punch that holds a number of needles, like the one shown (below). It is essential to use this with a sturdy foam block. These are sold at felting suppliers (see page 126) but an old garden kneeler would do just as well.

1. Start by taking a piece of organza and laying it on the block.

2. Press the needles into it and pull up the organza around the tool. This isn't exactly the way you are meant to use the tool but it is much the best way for an attack on the fabric. Pull the fabric away from the tool and repeat.

3. You will find that the weave of the fabric is broken by the barbs on the needles. Carry on until you have distorted the organza. You will also find that it is possible to distort some areas and leave others; this gives a contrast of rough and smooth surfaces.

4. Try lines of punching for a ruffled effect.

Two layers of chiffon were fused together with the hand needle punch. Care is needed as the needles are very sharp. Pull the fabric up around the tool, rather than pressing it into the chiffon. A lovely texture can be produced using this tool.

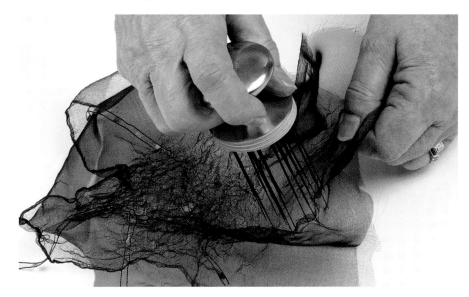

Do be aware how sharp the needles are and take great care. When you've gained sufficient confidence with this method, try:

- Layers of chiffon and organza with threads or snippets of fabric trapped between them.
- Wool, silk or nylon tops worked into a sheer fabric.
- Soft felt, used as a base with a sheer fabric on top.

You could also try using the heat gun on a distorted chiffon piece.

The Embellisher Machine

This machine looks, at first glance, like a sewing machine but it has a number of barbed needles, no thread and no bobbin. It is actually a mechanical version of the needle tool and is much faster and more versatile. It works with softer fabrics. Stiff papers or fabric can cause problems as they don't mesh and can break the needles. Make sure that the plastic ring is adjusted to be close to the fabric or, again, the needles may break. Try to form a habit of always lifting the lever at the back; don't be tempted to pull out the fabric without raising the needles and lifting this lever. Some fabrics work better than others: a background of commercial felt is particularly suitable. Place the layers under the needles, drop the lever and just 'stitch'. Work straight or form patterns as shown below.

Pieces of different fabrics laid on black net and embellished from the front and the back. Tiny loops of black show through on the front.

Ways of 'stitching' with the embellisher to make different surfaces and patterns.

You can use the Embellisher to:
- Distress chiffon and similar fine fabrics
- Bond fabrics together
- Trap yarns or anything else between fabric
- Apply non-woven yarns such as wool/nylon/silk tops
- Make and embellish ribbons
- Apply lace, motifs, stitch and so on
- Couch textured yarns for special effects
- Make a pattern on the top layer with chiffons.

Knitting tape laid on the front and back of black felt, and embellished on the front and the back to give strong and shadowy lines.

A background was created by embellishing silk tops over velvet lightly painted with gold paint. Commercial felt formed a backing. A layer of chiffon was placed over this and the Embellisher used in an up-and-down direction to form loose patterns. Free machined motifs were stitched on black felt, cut up and stitched over the background.

Work through the following using soft fabrics like chiffon, soft cottons, scrim or organza.

- Collect some bright strands of wool, nylon or silk tops and lay them on some dark commercial felt. 'Stitch' over them to see the results. Lift the needles, remove the fabric and look at the back. You'll find gentle drifts of colour.
- Now build up waves of colour using both sides of the felt to achieve a contrast of soft and solid effects. Try a textured yarn on top to add some definition; maybe stitch a grid.
- Note the way that the soft tops can be blended as they are applied. This will achieve subtle colour effects. How about a rainbow of colours running into each other? You can achieve this by blending the yarns where the two colours meet.
- For wonderful raised effects, form the wool or silk tops into shapes, perhaps triangles, on acrylic felt. Cut these out and use the heat tool to distort the felt a little and then embellish them back on top of a prepared background, just attaching them around the edge. This gives a cushioned effect.
- Make folds in a completed piece and run the needles along the edge. It will be 'stitched' together. Regular folds give a pintucked effect but random folds are also exciting.

Silk and wool tops were laid in strips over commercial felt and applied with the Embellisher. Chiffon formed the top layer and tucks were made to form areas where further embroidery will be applied.

Try the techniques on a variety of backgrounds using the soft silks, wool or nylon tops on such fabrics as silk paper. This gives a wonderful effect, especially on the reverse. It looks like moss stitch, so adding moss stitch over the top would be interesting.

Now try applying other materials. Patterned fabrics look great on the reverse as some of the pattern appears. A dark colour applied to a pale background fabric on the reverse gives a tattoo effect. With the right colours, this can look great.

Sheer Fabrics

Try stitching sheer fabric over organza with the Embellisher machine. The fabric will be wrecked and distressed, and it will look just wonderful. Then apply other sheer fabrics to the organza; chiffon is particularly suitable. Try trapping yarns or little bits of wool, nylon or silk tops between the two fabrics. Consider the direction in which you are 'stitching' and try circles, spirals or chevrons as shown in the diagram on page 93.

Take a piece of sheer fabric, a narrow strip, and run down one side of it. You will find that you have a frill. Then try stitching down the middle to see the different effects. You could also try applying these ribbon strips onto something like felt where they will ruche up as you stitch.

Two pieces of chiffon were embellished with small pieces of yarn trapped between them. This can now be placed on a background and the sewing machine used to produce a delicate embroidery.

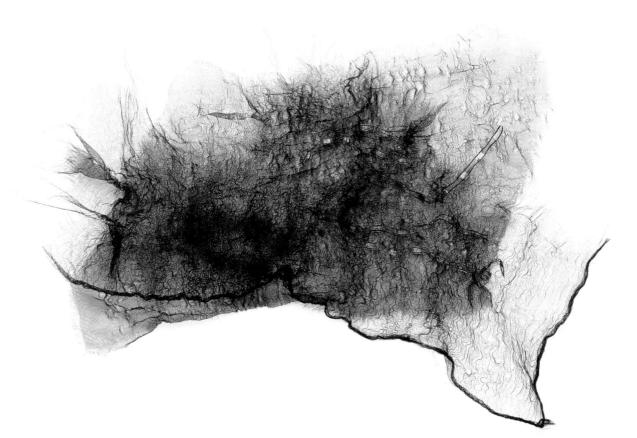

Very fine chiffon (the sort that the scarves are made from) has many uses. It works well for the following:

Black chiffon has been embellished through the layers with embedded gold leaf. Black felt is the background.

- Applying difficult fabrics. A stiff or painted cotton might be quite difficult to apply. However, if you lay it on the background and then cover it with chiffon, you will find when you stitch that you will not only achieve a slight haze of colour but that it will apply the more difficult fabric in a very satisfactory manner.

- Puff painting. Try stamping this on top of sheer fabric. Puff the paint using an iron and iron through baking paper (be careful here – if you use too much heat you won't have any fabric left). When the paint is puffed, apply the chiffon to a background or straight onto felt. Soften the edges by putting little bits of silk or wool tops over it and use the Embellisher to stitch it in.
- Laying scraps of lace on a background and using chiffon over the top. For a softer effect, try some slivers of silk tops over the lace. Alternatively, fold the chiffon so that it is heavier in some places than in others.

Holes

Changing the surface of the fabric by removing cut shapes from it and stitching the resulting hole will offer contrast.

Punching Holes

Some hole punches with interesting shapes are available from craft shops but even the humble office hole punch can be used with lacings for a decorative surface. The various shapes produced by hole punches offer unusual solutions for fastenings or decorated edges. Cut-out paper can be dipped in a Melting Pot, a piece of equipment that can be used for melting embossing powder (see page 113).

Try the following techniques.
- Punch holes in the fabric with an ordinary office hole punch before or after stitching. This gives the opportunity to thread wrapped cords (see page 63) or strips of fabric through the holes. This technique could be used for a panel edge, a book spine or built up in strips with other techniques.

Holes punched in embroidery on craft Vilene with zig zag cord laced through.

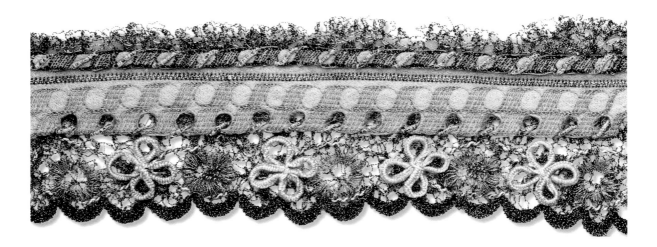

- Use decorative punches on paper, stiff Vilene (interfacing) or metal. If you use a sturdy handmade paper, it will be possible to stitch into it afterwards. Dipping the shapes into melted embossing powder is also possible. Alternatively, materials could be cut out with a punch and applied to a surface.

- Use one of the border punches with very fine metal foil or firm cartridge paper painted with metallic paints. Then couch through the holes to apply it to a background fabric.

Below: A punch was used to cut out flower shapes from fine metal shim. These were placed over velvet with a backing of craft Vilene and free machined. Strips of yarn were applied in rows between the flowers.

Below right: Three sail punches and a Japanese hole punch.

Right: Jane Wild found a hand-shape punch and used it on stiff paper. This also gave her a negative image that she tore out carefully. Both pieces were then dipped into a Melting Pot – see page 113.

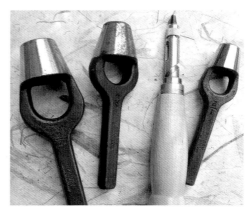

Punching Out

Sailmakers and bookbinders both use punches. Sewing machine accessories sometimes include small punches as part of the eyelet kit. Cut shapes from a piece of fabric. The fabric could be stitched first or the stitching could be built up afterwards. Work like this:

1. Choose a firm fabric for early experiments as the stitching will be easier. When you have got the feel for it, try it on previously stitched or softer fabrics. Punch out some holes, and save the cut-out pieces, which could then be put back on top.

2. Set the machine for satin stitch, foot off, teeth down. You could use the darning or free embroidery foot. Frame the fabric if you need to and stitch around the edges of the holes. If you have a Flower Stitcher attachment, stitch the circles first and cut them out afterwards.

Opposite, top: Automatic patterns were stitched with gold thread on white felt, which was edged with water-soluble lace. Holes were punched along the edge and cord laced through them.
(Jane Lemon)

Holes were punched inside satin stitched circles. The circles were created on the Flower Stitcher through trilobal nylon fibres and a layer of chiffon. More straight stitch circles were added, again using the Flower Stitcher. The organza and fibres were melted with a heat gun.

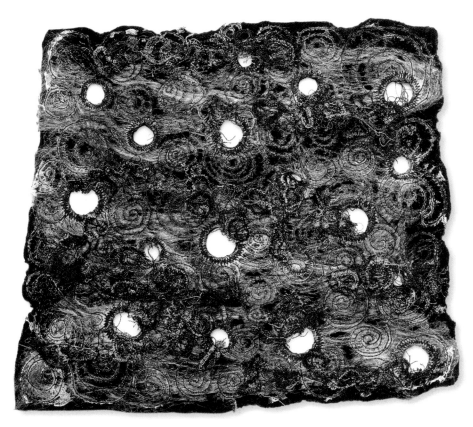

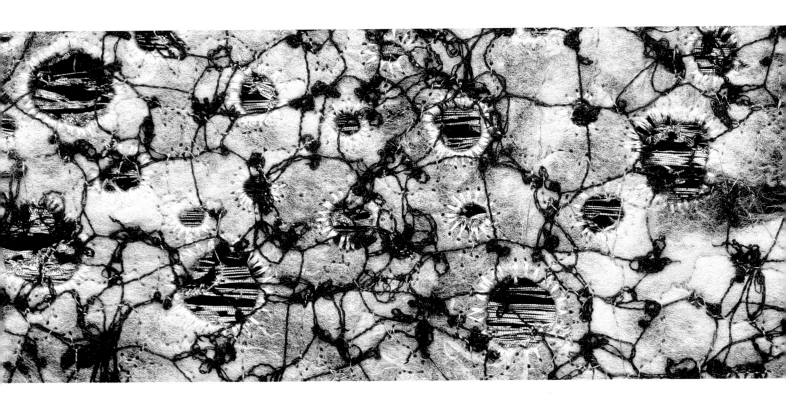

Large holes – punched through an embroidered piece – were strengthened with free satin stitch. Shredded metallic organza was placed behind the holes, and a web of water-soluble lace added on top.

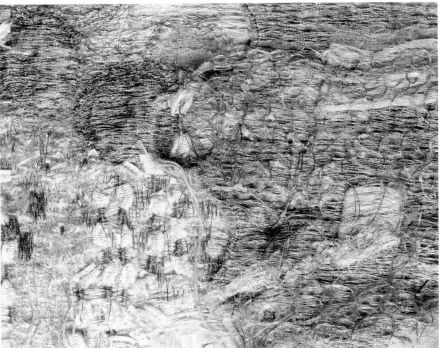

Large holes were punched out of a piece of embroidery and laid back on top. Further stitching secured the added pieces.

Melting the Fabric

The heat gun tool, used for melting and distressing synthetic fabrics, is no longer regarded as a curiosity but has become a part of the embroiderer's toolkit. You will need the more powerful heat guns for this as the smaller ones that look like mini hair dryers are not powerful enough. Paint strippers are often too hot, although some may work on the lowest setting. There are fabrics, such as Sizoflor, which can be stitched and distorted using heat. As well as giving a variety of textures for embroidery, these materials can be used for vessels, bowls and containers. They can be painted and gilded as required.

In this section, we cover:

- stitching on chiffon, organza and Sizoflor
- the use of embossing powders and ideas for applying them to fabric
- heating Thermogauze and heat-soluble fabrics after stitching to create a variety of effects.

Simple Melting

Most synthetic fabrics will react to heat, but care should be taken to wear a mask or, better still, a respirator when applying any heat to these fabrics. Some felts react really well to heat and an excellent result can be had by just stitching on the felt, leaving spaces between the stitching, and then zapping with the heat tool. An application of metallic wax can highlight the texture. Not all acrylic felts will work, though, as some may be fire-retardant. Trial and error is the only way to tell.

Chiffon

The right sort of acrylic chiffon (the fine scarves always work) can be stitched and then subjected to heat from a heat tool. The chiffon will almost disappear, except for that around the stitching, so the surface below will be revealed. Consider using this technique over velvet which has been coloured with metallic Markal (Shiva) oilbars.

1. Lay the decorated velvet over a firm soft backing. Felt is ideal as it will quilt a little. Place some ribbons, pieces of fabric or painted tissue on top, leaving gaps so that the background will show through. Place a piece of fine acrylic chiffon on top.

2. Free machine over this, considering marks such as circles or triangles. It should be firm enough to stitch without a frame but frame-up if necessary. Stitch more heavily in some areas and integrate the applied pieces well.

3. Play a heat tool over the surface of the piece, warming-up the tool away from the work and then gradually lowering it over the surface until the chiffon starts to react. Use a respirator, if possible, or work outside with a mask.

This technique could be varied by ironing fusible webbing onto parts of the velvet and applying Transfoil or sweet (candy) papers.

Chiffons and organzas were laid over background stitching. Shapes were stencilled on and filled with whip stitch. The fabrics were partially melted with a heat gun.

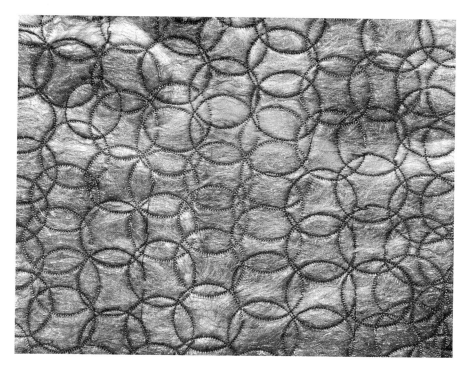

Left: Trilobal nylon fibres were laid on felt and covered with a chiffon scarf. Flower Stitcher circles in an overlapping pattern secured all the layers.

Below: A heat gun melted the chiffon, the fibres and some of the felt of the textile shown above.

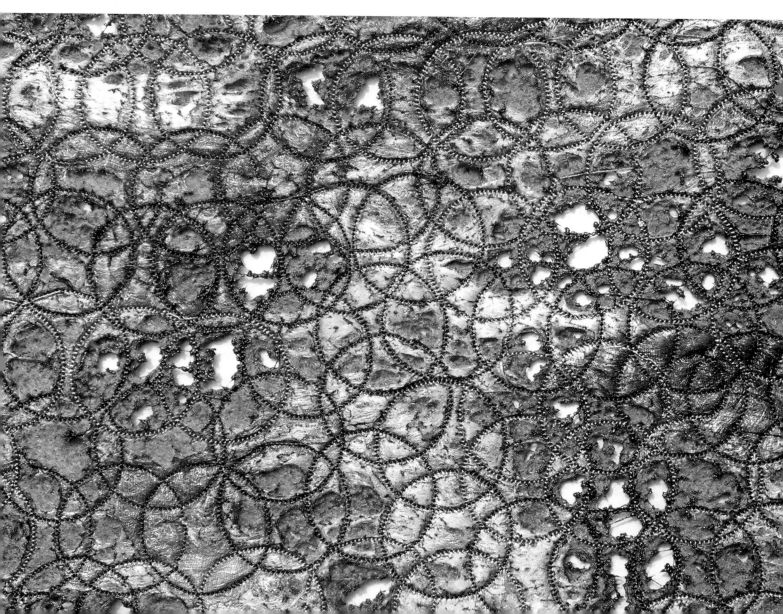

Metallic Organza

There is a particular type of fabric, often referred to as Indian organza, which is made from two different materials. One of these is impervious to heat while the other reacts really well and disappears when heated. This has obvious advantages. Just stitching a simple grid will give a piece of work with lovely long, loose threads. A square grid could be stitched with a motif, maybe a simple spiral, in the centre of some of the squares. When heated, the motif will hold the threads together. This fabric also works well stitched to a non-melting background.

1. Place a piece of the metallic organza over a cotton or silk fabric or one that will not be affected by the heat tool.

2. Stitch a design over the top of the organza. A defined pattern is better than a random one. Wide, built-in satin stitch patterns work well but, if you don't have them, try using the widest zigzag and pull it gently to and fro as you stitch.

Metallic organza was stitched to felt. The heat gun melted the warp threads leaving only the metallic weft threads. This was then placed over orange fabric and stitched to secure.

3. Use the heat tool to melt the top fabric and reveal the one below.

4. It could be interesting to stitch the underneath fabric before applying the organza.

Sizoflor

This is a material that is often used by florists or as fancy wrapping. The fabric has an interesting swirly texture and is quite open. It is available painted or unpainted (best painted after heating). If you paint it, be sure to place a piece of fabric underneath so as not to waste the paint. The paint can smoke when heated so dissolve first.

Use as for the chiffon (see page 103) or try trapping silk tops, threads, pieces of yarn or tiny snippets of fabric between two layers of Sizoflor. You may want to put it into a ring frame before doing some stitching to secure the trapped pieces. Then leave in the frame and warm gently with the heat gun, beginning with the nozzle raised and gradually lowering, as before. Try melting some areas and leaving others untouched.

Sizoflor can be melted over a shape (as seen in Julie Smith's work on page 108). Choose a shape made from heat-proof material and don't use glass or anything valuable. Lay the stitched piece over the shape and zap gently with the heat tool.

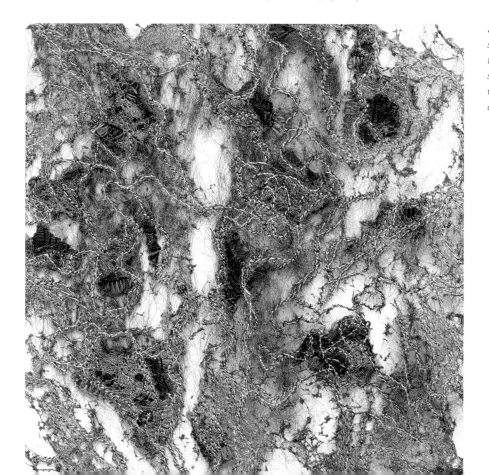

Snippets of fancy yarn and fine silk tops were trapped between two layers of Sizoflor. After stitching, they were heated gently with a heat gun to reveal the colour and texture below.

This delicate vessel was made from two layers of Sizoflor. These were lightly stitched before the fabric was placed over a shape and a heat gun used to shape the vessel and remove some of the fabric to give a light, lacy effect. Detail opposite. (Julie Smith)

Vanishing Muslin

This is a stiff, muslin-like fabric which becomes charred and crumbles away when heat is applied with a heat gun. It is a useful fabric for adding accents or incorporating in layering techniques. The material has a limited shelf life, so keep it away from light. The Thermogauze brand overcomes this problem as it keeps particularly well.

To use the muslin:

1. Stitch a design on the fabric, using patterns or free machine techniques. Do not stitch too heavily. Remember to allow space for removing the fabric.
2. Zap with a heat gun. Do not use too much heat or it will all crumble away. When heated, the material turns brown and crumbly and is easy to pull away. Try using less heat and catch it before the browning stage. Then pull apart with the fingers or tweezers.
3. When you are happy with the zapping, paint the fabric, using silk or fabric paints.
4. Apply to a background using hand stitching so as not to flatten the delicate muslin. Stab stitch to apply.

Painted Thermogauze was stitched to white fabric laid on black felt. It was burnt away using a heat gun.

One of the best ways to integrate the material into an embroidery is to stitch it in strips. These can be torn and then placed on a background fabric, perhaps velvet, and zapped. The material will cling to the stitching, giving a delicate effect. Alternatively, stitch the strips with a pattern, Flower Stitch circles or free machining. Zap the strips, paint them and then thread them through the gaps in one of the pieces made by pulling threads on waste canvas.

An interesting addition to the muslin is puff paint, which can be stamped or sponged on the vanishing muslin. Allow to dry and add a little stitching before puffing and crumbling the fabric.

Thermogauze was used to form a layered background in this embroidery. It was laid over painted fabric and stitched with a random pattern before being painted and zapped. A further piece of Thermogauze was stitched with a satin stitch pattern, painted and zapped and then machined on top. Finally, flower shapes were stitched on black felt, cut out and hand-stitched lightly to the background.

Painted Thermogauze was stitched to white fabric laid on black felt. It was burnt away using a heat gun.

Thermogauze was stamped with white puff paint before being zapped and painted. It was then applied to a painted brown paper background.

Embossing Powders

Embossing powders are often used to obtain raised effects with rubber stamps on paper. They can also be used much more freely. The Ultra Thick Embossing Enamel can create some great effects when melted down and used just on its own. The metallic shades are lovely but don't discount the interference colours, especially on dark surfaces. A simple but effective way of using them is to sponge acrylic felt with heat-safe paint (some metallic, acrylics paints are sold to use with embossing powders), sprinkle on the embossing powders and heat. The powders will add texture and the felt will melt a little. Cut up and apply to embroideries.

More ideas are set out below. Many of these will combine successfully with suggestions from earlier parts of the book.

Melting Techniques

A piece of equipment known as a Melting Pot is very useful if you become hooked on these embossing powder techniques. It is used with the thicker embossing powders known as UTEE (Ultra Thick Embossing Enamel). Pour it in and set the dial to UTEE. It will melt the UTEE and keep it at the right temperature to work with. If you want to try melting techniques before purchasing a Melting Pot, buy a deep metal ladle with a lip. Warm it by heating with a heat tool from underneath. Take care not to touch the bowl when it is hot. Just pour in some UTEE and heat, from below, to melt. Keep adding and melting until there is sufficient in the bowl. Check how it pours; you may need to hold the heat tool under it again if it starts to set.

1. Whichever method you use, melt the embossing powder in the Melting Pot or ladle.

2. Now put a small piece of glue stick – about 1 cm (½ in) – into the Melting Pot and 0.5 cm (¼ in) in the ladle. This makes it flexible when used with stitching. Otherwise it may be brittle.

3. Ink a rubber stamp, if required. The ink gives greater definition but is not strictly necessary. The long stamps called moulding mats or mini-moulding mats are the best ones to use here.

Ultra Thick Embossing Enamel (UTEE) is heated in a Melting Pot. It is then raised, using the handles, and slowly poured on to a rubber stamp, taking care with the hot liquid. When poured slowly in thin lines, the effect below can be achieved. This will quickly set and can be removed from the stamp.

4. Place the stamp on a sheet of baking paper, pour melted embossing powder onto the stamp, holding the pot or ladle high and pouring quickly so that you get streaks or drips on the stamp. Leave for a few minutes and peel away the stamp. The liquid doesn't damage the stamp but the very hot liquid may hurt you. Be very careful – especially if using a ladle – not to get a hand in the way. If you don't get the right effect by pouring, try using a spoon and pouring from that.

Attaching to Fabric

These 'drippy' pieces can be stitched onto fabric through the holes and thin gaps. Alternatively, try dripping straight onto fabric or a stitched piece.

Another good method of applying the stamped piece to fabric is to attach water-soluble paper while the enamel is hot. Work as instructions overleaf.

This embellished background was enhanced by the addition of Melting Pot stamps. The liquid embossing powder was backed with water-soluble paper before being removed from the stamp. The paper was made wet, allowed to dry and then couched on to the background.

1. Pour the melted powder from a ladle or Melting Pot onto a stamp.

2. Press a piece of water-soluble paper (slightly larger than the stamp) onto the embossing powder while it is on the stamp and still hot (see image below).

3. When cool, peel off the stamp and put both paper and stamped shape on another piece of water-soluble paper and then place on baking paper.

4. Paint with water to dissolve the paper until it turns to pulp. Push into a suitable shape around the motif.

5. Dry well and then stitch through the paper to a background.

6. Pressing a piece of scrim or organza onto the hot shape also works well. Felt will work too and will make a firmer piece. Try cutting it into tiles.

Placing the water-soluble paper on the melted embossing powder.

For this bracelet, built-in patterns were stitched on water-soluble film, ensuring an overlap to form a firm surface for embossing powder stamps. When it was dry, these were firmly stitched by hand to the dissolved base. Detail below.

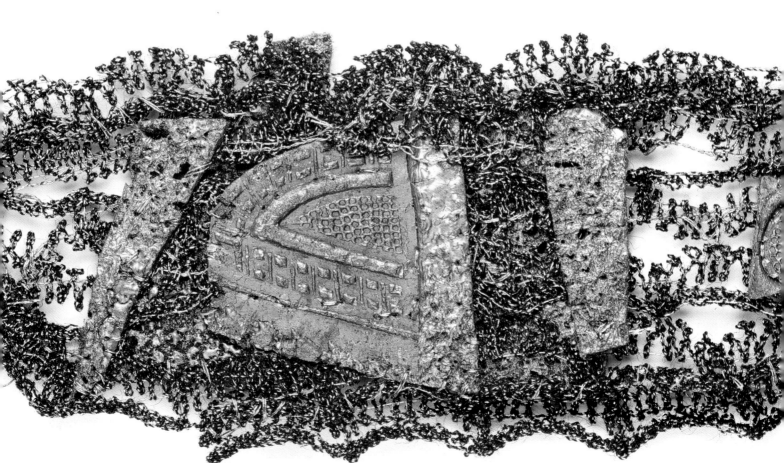

Dipped Fabrics

Try dipping pieces of lace, paper, stitching or anything else into the Melting Pot (this is not possible using the ladle). Really exciting effects can be achieved using a 'try anything' approach. Use tweezers to hold the piece that you are dipping. Small cut shapes can be edged using this method. Just hold with the tweezers and dip the edge in the pot. Lay on baking paper, allow to cool and then dip the next edge.

A 'dribbled' embossing powder stamp was backed by paper while still warm. A further piece of soft, black paper was dipped in the Melting Pot and placed behind it. The paper was stitched to an embellished background. Wrapped pipe-cleaners were used to complete the piece.

Opposite: Loose scrim was dipped in the Melting Pot, with further 'dripping' on top. Small tiles were made from thick, hand-made paper, also dipped in the Melting Pot and impressed with a rubber stamp while warm. The edges of the tiles were dipped in the pot, using tweezers to protect fingers.

Shaping the Fabric

In the next few pages, some suggestions are made for giving body to floppy, fragile work by using hardeners or stiffeners. This can be expanded into using a variety of media to give shape and add contours to embroidery or even to venture into three dimensions.

Adding Strength and Shape

Many of the techniques used in this book produce quite fragile textiles. The secret to preserving these pieces is to use a hardener to seal them and add durability. The hardener will also add shape to the embroidery and can even be used to form bowls or vessels.

This part of the book deals with:
- Hardening solutions which give a variety of effects from a gentle contour to a three-dimensional form.
- Wire, Wireform and shim, which offer exciting contrasts when used with stitch or combined with some of the effects described earlier; they can be manipulated by hand to produce many shapes and provide stunning effects.

Sculpture Glues and Hardeners

A variety of hardening solutions are available, which can be painted onto stitched fabric to allow the piece to be shaped and distorted. They will also protect the surface of the embroidery and give substance to a finished piece. A floppy textile can be given body using these preparations.

Three good products are available for this purpose:
- Blind Spray: a thin spray that must be painted on thickly or given two coats. It does rust pins but is fine on flat or three-dimensional pieces which will remain the same shape.
- Deco-Form: this is thicker and sometimes one coat will suffice. It rusts pins slightly.
- Paverpol: it comes in half-litre and one-litre containers. It is very similar to Deco-Form but does not rust pins at all. We find this is the best one.

All three are transparent when dry; can be mixed with bronze powders or acrylic paint to give a coloured but transparent effect; and can be painted afterwards.

Using the Hardeners

1. To distort a flat piece of embroidery, lay the piece on baking paper.

2. Now paint the hardening fluid onto the embroidery with a brush, ensuring that it is well covered.

3. Lift off the paper and place the piece on a sheet of expanded polystyrene, manipulating it to make the required shape. Pin it into shape and allow to dry.

Wireform

This is a flexible wire product which can be bought in a variety of weights and patterns. It comes in sheets or as a pack. The finer gauges can safely be stitched with the machine but it is safest to place fabric top and bottom to make sure that it doesn't scratch the sewing machine. There's a choice of metallic colours; this is useful if the product is to show through the stitching. It has very sharp edges and can really mangle your fingers so we recommend taping the cut edges before working with this product.

Wireform is great as a means of providing movement or shape for a piece of embroidery. It can be incorporated at an early stage but it is probably best sewn to the reverse of the work when most of the stitching is finished. At this stage the surface could be treated with a hardener such as Paverpol, which will protect the surface and prevent the Wireform from breaking.

1. Lay the completed embroidery on the Wireform with a fine fabric beneath it and stitch slowly, following the lines of the previous stitching.

2. When stitching is complete, bend the whole piece into the desired shape.

3. Form into boxes or vessels but try not to bend it too many times or it may break.

If you are nervous about using Wireform with the machine, it can be hand stitched when the work is completed. Take long stitches on the back and stab stitch up into the embroidery.

Acrylic felt could be laid on top of the Wireform and stitched. The felt could then be zapped with a heat tool, allowing some of the wire to show through.

Commercial felt embellished with silk tops formed the background for this embroidery. Painted polycotton was embellished on top and applied using a chiffon scarf. The piece was then placed on Wireform and stitching used to both enhance the piece and to give it shape.

A variation on this might be to lay painted silk over the wire and stitch, place the felt on top, do some more stitching and then use the heat tool. The felt will melt to show the stitched silk, which should resist the heat. Bend the wire to give movement.

We hope that this book has given you some new ideas in stitching, dissolving and manipulating your work. We really feel that, with many of the techniques described, we are only beginning to explore the possibilities, so there are lots more excitements to be discovered.

Detail of cloth with cross-hatched stitching on the base fabric, with areas worked on the Embellisher. Motifs were stitched and laid over crumpled organza.

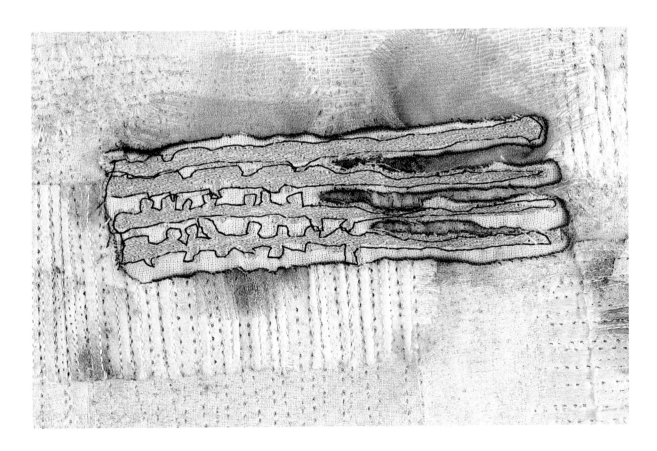

The background to this work is Sizoflor, stitched to velvet and zapped. Motifs were stitched on Thermogauze, painted and zapped before being applied to the embroidery. Borders were made from acrylic felt, stitched on Wireform and zapped. These were formed into ridges with coils of wire threaded with wrapped pipe-cleaners.

suppliers

Art Van Go, The Studios,
1 Stevenage Road, Knebworth,
Herts SG3 6AN
Tel: 01438 814946
Email: art@artvango.co.uk
Website: www.artvango.co.uk
*Paints, Paverpol, transfer paints, silk and
Kozo fibres, Stiffen Stuff, metallic wax,
Wireform, Wiremesh, Xpandaprint, heat
tool, Markal (Shiva) oil bars*

Barnyarns, Canal Wharf, Bondgate
Green, Ripon, North Yorkshire
HG4 1AQ
Tel: 01765 690069
Email: info@barnyarns.com
Website: www.barnyarns.com
*Water-soluble film, fabrics and paper,
threads, sticky stabilizer, 505*

Craftsmistress, 66 Green Lane,
Ockbrook, Derby DE7 23SE
Tel: 01332 67894
Email: flora@craftsmistress.co.uk
Website: www.craftsmistress.co.uk
Water-soluble film

David Drummond
77–81 Haymarket Terrace, Edinburgh
EH12 5HD
Tel: 0131 5397766
Sewing machines, Babylock Embellisher

Franklyn's, 48 Fisherton Street,
Salisbury, Wilts SP7 2RB
Tel: 01722 322770
*Sewing machines, haberdashery,
Babylock Embellisher*

Gillsew, Boundary House, Moor
Common, Lane End, Bucks
HP14 3HR
Tel: 01494 881886
Email: gillsew@ukonline.co.uk
*Waste canvas, water-soluble film, felt,
heat tool, 505 spray*

Stewart Gill, 20 Lochrin Buildings,
Edinburgh EH3 9NB
Email: enquiries@stewartgill.com
*Rubber stamps, heat-safe paints,
embossing powders, etc.*

Ivy House Studio, 37 High Street,
Kessingland, Suffolk NR33 7QQ
Email: ivyhousestudio@hotmail.com
*Melting Pot, water-soluble film and
paper, surface decoration supplies
including embossing powders, heat tool,
Taggar Paints, 505 spray*

Oliver Twists, 22 Phoenix Road,
Crowther, Washington,
Tyne & Wear NE38 0AD
Tel: 01914 166016
Email: jean@olivertwists.freeserve.co.uk
*Hand-dyed variegated machine
embroidery threads, silk tops, other threads*

Rainbow Silks, 85 High Street,
Great Missenden, Bucks HP16 0AL.
Mail order from 6 Wheelers Yard, High
Street, Great Missenden,
Bucks HP16 0AL
Tel: 01494 862111
Email: caroline@rainbowsilks.co.uk
Website: www.rainbowsilks.co.uk
*Paints, stencils, printing blocks, water-
soluble film and paper, heat tool, Melting
Pot, Sizoflor, moulding mats*

Sewmaster, 3 West Street, Reading,
Berks RG1 1TT
Tel: 01189 571845
Website: www.sewmaster.com
Sewing machines and accessories

Stamp Attic, 9 Arbery Arcade,
Market Place, Wantage, Oxfordshire
OX12 8AB
Tel: 01235 760821
Email: Wendy@thestampattic.co.uk
Website: www.thestampattic.co.uk
Adirondack color wash sprays

Tim Parker, 124 Corhampton Road, Bournemouth, Dorset BH6 5NZ
Tel: 01202 429455
Fine lace threads

T C Threads Ltd, Mancor House, Bolsover Street, Hucknell, Notts NG15 7TZ
Tel: 01159 680089
Machine embroidery threads, fine coloured bobbin threads, 505

The Textile Directory
Email: orders@textiledirectory.com
Website: www.thetextiledirectory.com
Directory of embroiderers' courses, suppliers

Twist Fibre Craft, 88 High Street, Newburgh, Fife KY14 6AQ
Tel: 01337 842843
Email: enquiries@twistfibrecraft.co.uk
Website: www.twistfibrecraft.co.uk
Felting needle punch, wool tops and fibres

Winifred Cottage, 17 Elms Road, Fleet, Hants GU51 3EG
Tel: 01252 617667
Email: winifcott@aol.com
Water-soluble film, fabrics and paper, threads, waste canvas, felt, chiffon scarves, acrylic fibres, 505, Thermogauze

New Zealand
Craft Supplies, 31 Gurney Road, Belmont, Lower Hutt, New Zealand
Most supplies

North America
Most materials in this book are available from haberdashers, including water-soluble film, fabrics and paper.

American Art Clay Co
Website: www.amaco.com
Wireform, Wiremesh, shim

Clearsnap Inc, PO Box 98, Anacortes, WA 98221, USA
Email: Linda.Brown@clearsnapinc.com
Moulding mats

Embroidery Adventures
Email: reliker@embroideryadventures.com
Most supplies

Impress Me
Website: www.impressmenow.com
Impress Me stamps by Sherrill Kahn

Meinke Toy, PMB#411, 55 E Long Lake Road, Troy MI 48085, USA
Email: info@meinketoy.com
Most supplies

Australia
The Thread Studio, 6 Smith Street, Perth, WA 6000, Australia
Tel: 61 (0)9 227 1561
Email: dale@thethreadstudio.com
Website: www.thethreadstudio.com
Most supplies

index